FOREST PROTECTION

Guide to Lectures
Delivered at the Biltmore Forest School
by

C. A. SCHENCK, Ph. D.
Director.

1909

The Inland Press,
Asheville, N. C.

PREFACE

This book on "forest protection" is being printed, pre-eminently, for the benefit of the students attending the Biltmore Forest School.

In American forestry, the most important duty of the forester consists in the suppression of forest fires.

If forest fires were prevented, a second growth would follow invariably in the wake of a first growth removed by the forester or by the lumberman; and the problem of forest conservation would solve itself.

If forest fires were prevented, a second growth would have a definite, prospective value; and it would be worth while to treat it sylviculturally.

If forest fires were prevented, our investments made in merchantable timber would be more secure; and there would be a lesser inducement for the rapid conversion of timber into cash.

The issue of forest fires stand paramount in all forest protection. Compared with this issue, the other topics treated in the following pages dwindle down to insignificance.

I write this with a knowledge of the fact that the leading timber firms in this country place an estimate of less than 1% on their annual losses of timber due to fires:

These firms are operating close to their holdings; and if a tract is killed by fire the operations are swung over into the burned section as speedily as possible; and the salvage may amount to 99% of the timber burned.

These firms do not pay any attention, in their estimate, to the "lucrum cessans," nor to the prospective value of inferior trees, poles, saplings and seedlings.

The "prospective forest" is the forest of the future; and this forest is annihilated by the fires.

Merchantable trees of immediate value cannot be killed any "more dead" by fires, nor by insects, nor by strom, than by the legitimate use of axe and saw.

Where the means of transportation are ready, the damage inflicted upon the forest and upon its owner by catastrophies may be reduced to a minimum.

In writing the paragraph on "forest insects," I have availed myself of many hints obtained from Dr. A. D. Hopkins. My own knowledge of forest insects amounts to little; and on the basis of past experience, I strongly recommend to all foresters a "lack of self-reliance" in forest entomological questions. Consult Dr. Hopkins before spending any money for fighting insects!

Mr. C. D. Couden has revised and rewritten my manuscript on forest insects, eliminating many mistakes made by a layman. My sincerest thanks are tendered to him herewith.

Whatever I know of American tree diseases and of timber diseases induced by fungi, I have learned from Dr. Hermann von Schrenk. The errors only which may have crept into the 7th paragraph of this book dealing with fungus diseases are my own

The graduates of the Biltmore Forest School, and all other gentle readers are earnestly requested to assist me in the elimination of errors and mistakes contained in this book on forest protection.

Biltmore, N. C., October 1, 1909. C. A. SCHENCK.

FOREST PROTECTION

DEFINITION AND SYNOPSIS.

The term "Forest Protection" comprises all the acts of the forest-owner made with a view to the safety of his investments.

Forest Protection as a branch of science is divided into the following parts and chapters:

PART A: Protection Against Organic Nature.

Chapter I: Protection against man.
Chapter II: Protection against animals.
Chapter III: Protection against plants.

PART B: Protection Against Inorganic Nature.

Chapter I: Protection against adverse climatic influences.
A—Heat.
B—Frost.
C—Snow and sleet.

Chapter II: Protection against storm, erosion, sanddrifts, noxious gases.
D—Wind and storm.
E—Erosion.
F—Shifting sand.
G—Noxious gases.

The English literature on Forest Protection consists, in the main, of the following:

Dr. Wm. Schlich, Vol. IV. of "Manual of Forestry."

Dr. A. D. Hopkins, Bulletins of the West Virginia Agricultural Station. Bulletins of the U. S. Bureau of Entomology.

Tubeuf and Smith, "Diseases of Plants."

Dr. H. von Schrenk, bulletins of the Shaw School of Botany, bulletins of the U. S. Bureau of Forestry and of the U. S. Bureau of Plant Industry.

Lectures on game protection, on protection of forest-roads and forest-railroads, on protection of forest industries—of vital interest to the owner of forests—are not included in the following paragraphs. The author's excuse for this omission lies in the word "precedent."

CONTENTS IN PARAGRAPHS.

Part A: Protection Against Organic Nature

CHAPTER 1. PROTECTION AGAINST MAN.

Par. 1. Protection Against Adverse Possession.

Adverse possession and its consequences are best prevented by continuous, open and notorious possession of every acre of land comprised in the property. To that end, a proper survey is necessary, coupled with demarkation of the boundary lines by proper marks or by fences; of the corners by proper corner trees and witnesses.

Wooden stakes as corner signs are objectionable; iron "T" stakes, 5' long, costing 35 to 60 cents apiece, are extensively used at Biltmore.

The exactness of the survey depends on the acre-value of the forest.

The lines of the property, established by the demarkation, must be maintained by continuous patrolling. The posting of trespass notices and the trimming of bushes along the lines are advisable, if not legally required. Foremen, tenants and guards should know the lines perfectly so as to be witnesses available in lawsuits.

In the case of disputes with neighbors, refuge to "processioning proceedings" is taken.

The forester should endeavor to straighten the lines of the forest by purchase or exchange, and to substitute natural boundary lines for artificial lines.

Squatters, with the help of state grants or other colorable title,—or without title but with distinct boundary lines and with distinct possession—become owners within a few years.

In real estate law, the WRITTEN word is decisive rather than the gist of a contract.

The lessee surrenders to the lessor all claim to the property on which he lives.

All deeds pertaining to a piece of property should be placed on public record.

Suit should be brought in the federal courts, preferably.

In the distant future, the increased value of real property will force the states to "legalize" the individual holdings after careful survey.

The administering forester must command a good knowledge of real estate law; he should leave no means untried to ferret out the trespasser and to secure his conviction.

The most important laws in this connection are those concerning

Destruction of corner marks
Larceny of wood and timber
Entering land when forbidden
Arrest
Proceedings at court.

Par. 2. Protection Against Forest Fires.

Protection against forest fires means, practically, protection against man who, intentionally or carelessly, causes the very large majority of all forest fires. Fires due to lightning are of rare occurrence in the East.

A: CAUSES OF FIRES:

I:—Fires are intentionally set:—

To improve pasture.
To uncover minerals for prospecting.
To gather chestnuts.
To force the owner of woodlands to purchase interior holdings.
To chase deer or turkeys.
To drive bees or coons from trees.
To improve the huckleberry crop.
To facilitate access to thick woods.
To get a job at stopping fires.
To surround farms, pastures or forests with a safety belt of burned land.
To mask trespass by fishing and hunting.
To take revenge for supposed acts of animosity.

II:—Fires carelessly started result from:—

Locomotive sparks and cinders.
Sparks from forest cabins.
Campers' and hunters' fires.
Charcoal burning, rock blasting, tobacco smoking, burning adjoining fields or pastures.

B: KINDS OF FOREST FIRES:

Fires are distinguished as:—

Surface fires.
Underground fires.
Top fires.

C: DAMAGE BY FIRES:

The damage done by forest fires consists of the loss of present values or of the loss of prospective values; seedlings are killed; saplings burst open; stool shoots replace seedling growth.

A heavy growth of weeds, frequently following in the wake of forest fires, prevents natural or artificial regeneration. A deterioration of productiveness is the natural consequence of deteriorated soil, due to destruction of humus.

Trees weakened by fires cease to resist the attacks of insects and fungi. Trees burned at the stump are subject to breakage by sleet or snow.

D: The Factors Influencing the Amount of Damage are:—

The age of the woods.

The aspect of the slope.

The severity of the wind, and the uphill or downhill direction of the wind.

The season of the year and the preceding duration of drought.

The silvicultural system.

The amount of débris and humus on the ground.

The species forming the forest (conifers have less reproductive power; light demanders usually have fireproof armor of bark; thin or thick layer of sap wood.)

E: The Measures Taken Against Forest Fires are Either of a Preventive or of a Remedial Nature.

I.—Preventive measures:—

Education of the people and of the legislature through the newspapers and from the pulpit.

Friendly relations with all neighbors.

Securing proper fire laws and publishing notices giving the essence of such laws.

The purchase of all interior holdings.

Settlements of tenants within the forest.

Telephone connection in the forest.

Fire lanes (in India up to 400′ wide) kept clear from inflammable material. Such lanes exist along all European railroads. In America the main advantage of a fire lane lies in the possibility of back firing with the lane as a basis.

Trails or roads, further strips of pasture along the ridges and strips of farmland along the creeks form the most useful fire lanes.

Burning all around the forest at the beginning of the dangerous season.

Burning débris after lumbering—a measure of doubted expediency.

Removing débris from the close proximity of valuable trees.

Proper contracts for all work in the woods by which the liability for damage caused by fires is thrown upon the contractor.

Annual burning of the woods intended to prevent the accumulation of vegetable matter or mould. (Pineries of the South).

Removing duff from the close proximity of turpentine boxes.

Stock law.

Associations of forest owners, as in Idaho, Washington and Oregon.

Pasture by cattle and hogs to cause a more rapid decomposition of the vegetable carpet.

Unceasing patrol of the forest during the dry season or during dry spells, day and night, by an increased staff of watchmen, thoroughly acquainted with their beat and with the people living in the neighborhood.

II.—Remedial Measures:—

a.—Main principles:—

Have one man in full charge and hold him alone responsible.

Have helpers and relays for helpers ready in the various ranges (*scattering the work*) during droughts, employing them in lumbering or in silviculture until their help is required at a fire.

The foreman, upon arrival at the fire, must first ascertain the speed of the fire and the length of the line of attack; further, the distance from the next fire lane (trail, brook, pasture), and the amount of help locally available.

The foreman must not hesitate to abandon the burning district, up to the next or second next fire lane.

Food and water for the fire-fighters must be provided.

The fire is subdued only when the last spark is extinguished. The edges of the burned area must be watched for 24 hours succeeding the fire.

b.—Tools:—

The axe, hoe, spade, shovel, rake (preferably wooden teeth); brooms; plows on abandoned fields; water buckets and sprinkling cans; pack-train, or railroad-velocipedes properly equipped; fire extinguishers.

c.—Actual Work:

(1) Underground fires can be stopped only by digging ditches and by turning water into them.

(2) Surface fires are stopped

By plowing or digging a furrow around the fire.

By beating the fire out with brooms or green twigs.

By removing the humus and débris from a narrow line in front of the fire by hand or rake.

By throwing dirt on the fire.

By sprinkling in front of the fire.

By the use of extinguishers against the flame itself.

By back-firing from the next point of vantage with due regard for the speed of the fire—the best and only remedy in the case of heavy conflagrations.

(3) Top fires can be stopped only by providing broad fire lanes on which the trees are cut, and by back-firing from such lanes.

(4) Stem fires burning in hollow trees are stopped by filling the holes in the trunk with dirt or by cutting the tree down.

Fires going down hill, against the wind and in the hours following midnight are the easiest to subdue.

For the history of some famous forest fires, see Pinchot's Primer, Part I.

For a number of tree species (notably Douglas fir, Yellow pines, Jack pine, Lodgepole pine, Aspen) fire must be considered as an excellent silvicultural tool or as a means of securing regeneration.

F:—Treatment of Injured Woods.

The treatment of injured woods differs according to species, age of woods, market facilities and severity of damage inflicted.

I—Thickets of broadleaved species it is best to coppice, or else to clip down with the help of long handled pruning shears.

Thickets of conifers are either so badly damaged as to require regeneration anew or are so little damaged as not to require any help.

II—Pole Woods.

Pole woods of broadleaved species are most severely damaged by spring fires, and should be cut where salable.

Pole woods of conifers, if apt to die, should be made into money immediately, where possible.

If coniferous pole woods are apt to live, careful trap-tree practice will tend to avoid more severe injury from insect plagues.

III.—Tree Forests.

Broadleaved tree forests are not apt to be injured by surface fires sufficiently to cause the death of the trees. Hence, usually, the trees are allowed to stand. If, however, a majority of the trees are killed, speedy utilization is necessary.

In coniferous tree forests, trees are either at once killed by the fire, requiring immediate removal, or else not sufficiently touched to be doomed. In the latter case, the use of trap trees is required to prevent insect plagues from developing.

The presence of permanent means of transportation connecting the forest with a ready market is, under all circumstances, the most important factor in preventing material damage from striking the owner of merchantable forests killed by conflagrations.

CHAPTER II: PROTECTION AGAINST ANIMALS.

Par. 3. Protection Against Domestic Animals on Pasture.

A—INTRODUCTION.

Forest pasture is a legitimate forest industry. The waste production of the soil, in addition to shoots and branches of trees, are utilized by pasturing stock Vegetable matter transformed into flesh or wool adopts a more marketable and a more profitable shape.

Forest pasture is, obviously, best adapted to woods of low stumpage prices; of difficult access; of scant timber production (East slopes of the Cascades, ridge between Pisgah and Balsam mountains).

Forest pasture plays a role in the forest similar to that which field pasture plays on the farm.

Whether forest pasture pays better in connection with tree growth or regardless of timber production,—that is a financial question to be answered by every land owner on the basis of local experience and of individual forecast.

Abroad, since times immemorial, forests have been pastured and are still pastured to a surprising extent

Pasture frequently acts as a silvicultural tool; hogs are used to break the soil and to destroy insects; cattle or sheep driven over seed plantations or through the woods after seed-fall imbed the seeds to a proper depth; they destroy rank weeds overshadowing valuable seedlings.

B—THE DAMAGE BY PASTURE IN THE FOREST IS THREEFOLD:—

I.—To soil Pasture hardens hard soil and loosens loose soil.

II.—To trees. This damage consists of:

a.—Browsing on buds, leaves and shoots.

b.—Eating seeds and uprooting seedlings.

c.—Tramping down seedlings and over-riding saplings.

d.—Tossing-off the tops of saplings.

e.—Peeling hardwood poles in spring.

III.—To roads and road drainage.

C.—FACTORS OF DAMAGE ARE:

I.—Species of trees: Those most exposed are ash, maple, locust, chestnut, linden, elm; less exposed are yellow poplar, willows, oaks (horses like oaks), birch, fir, hickory and walnut; least endangered are larch, spruce, pine. Practically safe is red cedar.

II.—Age of trees: The seedling stage suffers most.

III.—Silvicultural system: Systems in which the age classes are mixed suffer most, notably selection system and group system.

IV.—Locality: Steep slope, loose soil and shifting sand suffer severely.

V.—Species of animals: The animals may be arranged in the following schedule, placing the damage done by a horse at 100:

Horse or mule foal	150
Horse or mule	100
Yearling cattle	75
Grown cattle	50
Goats	25
Sheep	10

Since a goat weighs 80 lbs. and a horse 10 times as much, the damage done by the goat is relatively great. In addition, goats prefer woody shoots and buds to mere grass.

The rates charged for forest pasture in Pisgah Forest correspond more or less with this schedule, viz:

Horses	90 cents per head per month
Cattle	50 cents per head per month
Sheep	10 cents per head per month

In the pineries of the South, the lease receipts from pasture offset the taxes frequently. Foals destroy pasture more by their mere frolics than by their appetite. After Hundeshagen, 10 to 12½ acres of forest are required for the pasture of one head of cattle.

VI.—Season of the year. Spring pasture is more destructive than summer or fall pasture.

D.—Closed Time.

In Central Europe young woods are closed to pasturage for a number of years.

AGE OF WOODS WHEN PASTURE BEGINS, IN YEARS.

SPECIES OF ANIMALS	HIGH FOREST, BROAD LEAF	HIGH FOREST, CONIFERS	COPPICE FOREST
Horses	18 to 24	12 to 20	6 to 14
Cattle	14 to 18	9 to 16	4 to 10

E.—Duration of Pasture

In Western North Carolina, cattle are pastured in the woods from May 1st, to October 15th, whilst sheep and hogs are kept on pasture during the entire year, fed only slightly after a heavy snow fall.

In the pineries of the South, cattle, sheep and hogs are kept in the woods during the entire year. Cattle are fed slightly, in addition to the pasture, during the four winter months. The much disputed pasture in the Sierras and Cascades is used only during the three summer months when the pasture in the lowlands dries out.

F.—PASTURE IN THE NATIONAL FORESTS:

The pasture of sheep and goats is generally prohibited; cattle pasture generally allowed.

Sheep ranges and cattle ranges are kept strictly apart

The Secretary of Agriculture determines annually the amount of pasturage permitted for each forest, viz:

a.—The number of horses, cattle, sheep and goats to be admitted;

b—The beginning and the end of the grazing season;

c—The ranges actually to be grazed.

The stock of residents owning holdings within the forests is given preference over "neighboring stock" Only citizens of the State are entitled to grazing privileges.

Under any circumstances, permits must be obtained through the supervisor by stock owners intending to pasture on the reserve (the stock of travelers and prospectors excepted). Sheep must be herded by a herdsman.

The sheep ranges are allotted separately, usually according to the recommendation of the local Wool Growers' Association. Promiscuous sheep grazing is strictly prohibited.

Permit holders are required to prevent and to fight fires without compensation.

G.—PROTECTIVE MEASURES MEANT TO SAFEGUARD THE TIMBER INTERESTS OF THE LAND OWNER—

I.—Animals:

a.—Limit the number of animals admitted.

b.—Exclude goats.

c.—Prevent cattle from following sheep.

II.—Time:

a.—Prevent pasture in early spring.

b.—Insist on close time during regeneration and up to the thicket stage.

c.—Close forest pasture periodically so as to allow tree seedlings to escape the mouth of browsing animals.

III.—Fencing:

For cattle pasture, two or three strings of barbed wire are sufficient. For sheep pasture three or four strings 100 lbs. of barbed wire form a string 1,600 to 1,900 feet long.

Individual trees or seedlings, like orchard trees, are sometimes protected by screens placed around the tree.

IV.—Seedlings should be planted within the "bays" of tree stumps after clear cutting wherever artificial regeneration is resorted to. Seed planting should be avoided.

Par. 4. Protection Against Wild Vertebrates.

Amongst the wild animals preying upon the forest the mammals figure as well as the birds. The role played by the vertebrates in the "household" of the forest is little known.

Birds and mammals may injure the forest directly—by eating vegetable matter produced in the forest,—or indirectly—by killing the friends of the forester. Utility of a wild animal is frequently combined with noxiousness, e. g. in the case of the crow, blue-jay, fox.

Useful animals may help the forester either directly—by seed distribution,—or indirectly—by killing the enemies of the forest.

A.—Protection Against Mammals Forming the Object of Chase.

I.—Deer.

a.—The damage done consists in:—

Eating fruits

Browsing on shoots and seedlings

Peeling the bark of saplings and poles (notably of spruce, oak, ash).

Rubbing off the bark when freeing the antlers of velvet.

Tramping down plantations or natural regenerations.

The objects of damage are, above all, the rare species, or species arousing the curiosity of the deer.

b.—Protective measures are:—

Proper regulation of the number of deer. Compatible with the objects of silviculture are, per 10,000 acres, 50 head of elk or 150 head of Virginia deer, provided that nurseries are fenced.

Feeding during winter by cutting soft woods or by providing hay stacks. Mast-bearing trees should be encouraged; grass meadows should be maintained, a few patches should be planted in turnips, potatoes, clover, etc. Maintaining salt licks, especially with a view to preventing bark peeling in spring. Hohlfeld's game powder is said to answer the purpose still better. Fencing nurseries and young growth.

Sprinkling seedlings with kerosene, liquid manure, blood, cotton residue or, better, covering the fall shoots, exclusive of bud, with coal tar. Coal tar is especially effective in the case of fir and spruce. Thinnings should be delayed as long as possible. Planting is preferable to sowing, especially to sowing in the fall.

II.—Wild Boar. Boar are particularly disastrous to nurseries, natural regenerations and plantations. The only remedies are strong fences.

III.—HARES AND RABBITS. The damage done consists in the biting-off of top shoots (notably of oaks, maples, firs, but also of pine); further, in gnawing-off the bark of locust, cratægus, cherry, hard maple, linden.

At Biltmore, rabbits feast especially on the shoots of the Buffalo nut (Pyrularia) The seedlings of Pinus echinata, in certain years, were bitten-off in the nurseries.

Plantations of acorns at Biltmore have been annihilated by the rabbits, the shoots being clipped year after year. Thus the oak seedlings were prevented from successfully competing with the weeds (broom sedge). Nurseries require a fine meshed fence. Remedies lie, above all, in the protection of the fox, 'possum, skunk, marten, weasel, hawk, coon, mynx.

In addition, sprinkling with coal tar (not on buds!) and wrapping of top shoots in cotton waste is recommended.

The planting of rabbit-proof species (notably Picea pungens and Picea Sitchensis) is advisable.

B.—PROTECTION AGAINST MAMMALS WHICH DO NOT FORM THE OBJECT OF THE CHASE.

Obviously, all carniverous animals are friends of the forester, whilst most herbivorous animals appear as his enemies. Amongst the plant eaters, the rodents excel in the amount of harm done.

I.—SQUIRRELS.

a.—Damage done.

Squirrels eat the seed on the tree as well as the seed planted by nature and man, preferring sweet oaks, beech, chestnut, walnut, cucumber-tree, hickories, pines. They eat the cotyledons, buds and cambium of young shoots and destroy the nest brood of some useful birds. In the Pink Beds, the top shoots of white pine are cut off by the squirrels. Plantations of the heavy seeded broad leaved species have been destroyed at Biltmore repeatedly.

b.—Protective measures.

Protect the fox, marten, skunk, coon, o'possum, hawk, owl, cat (wild and tame) and all other enemies.

Remove hollow trees forming the hiding and nesting places of the squirrel.

Plant seedlings or, possibly, nuts after sprouting, and if seeds must be planted, resort to spring-planting of the same.

c.—Remedial measures.

1—Shoot the squirrel

2—Poison it by bathing the seeds in strychnine before planting, a means found ineffective at Biltmore.

II.—CHIPMUNK. Similar damage and same remedies as for the squirrel. Its main enemy at Biltmore is the black snake and the rattlesnake.

III.—Mice.

a.—Damage done.

The mice live on buds, seeds, seedlings and the cambium layers of seedlings.

The field mice undermine the ground in nurseries and plantations following the rows of plants and cutting the roots about one inch below the surface of the ground. Frequently they seem to follow in mole mines. The damage done by gnawing is conspicuous in plantations of locust and black cherry. In seed plantations on abandoned fields at Biltmore, mice have done enormous damage to oaks and hickories. Planted locusts are bitten-off below ground. In the Biltmore nurseries, oak seed beds have suffered severely by the mice cutting the roots. Transplanted white pines were severely decimated, by girdling, in February, 1909.

b.—Protective measures.

Avoid autumn sowing.

Plant seeds broadcast instead of planting in rills

Have nurseries far from grain fields and from abandoned fields. Keep deep and clean pathways between the beds. Surround nurseries by deep and steep-walled trenches. Insert pit falls in the bottom of such trenches. Work the nurseries continuously. Do not cover the nurseries with mould or moss forming hiding places.

Keep the sedge grasses and weeds down in nurseries and regenerations, possibly by pasturing with cattle and sheep, thus disturbing the mice and tramping down their mines. Burn abandoned fields before planting

Pigs admitted to the woods just before a seed year destroy the mice whilst preparing the soil for natural regeneration. Protect the mouse-eaters, especially those which are fond of voles as owls, crows, fox, o'possum, cats.

c.—Remedial Measures.

Kill the mice by trapping or poisoning. In this latter case, place grains of wheat poisoned by immersion in strychnine, arsenic or phosphorus into drain pipes so as to check the possibility of accidentally poisoning singing birds or quail at the same time. Comp Farmers bulletin No. 369, Biological Survey. The root of certain Scylla species, chopped into sausages, kills the mice by causing their bladders to burst. Gypsum is said to have a similar effect, solidifying in the stomach. The latter remedies are not injurious to the mouse-eating animals which are frequently poisoned by catching the poisoned mice. The vaccination of the mice with the so-called "typhoid disease" has not been sufficiently successful so far.

d.—Treatment of injured plants.

Broad leaved seedlings merely chewed above ground should be clipped back. Oak seedlings, cut off below ground, have been successfully transplanted at Biltmore and have replaced the lost tap-root by a multitude of rootlets.

IV.—Ground Hog or Wood Chuck. Dr. Fernow reports that his coniferous nurseries at Axton were badly plundered by woodchuck. After Schaaf, white oak saplings are peeled by woodchucks up to five feet from the ground, near fields. Stomach analysis at Biltmore show only ferns.

V.—Porcupine or Hedgehog. It peels the bark, especially that of spruce, basswood and hemlock, close to the base of the tree, preferring saplings up to 5″ in diameter.

VI.—Beaver. It is now so rare that the damage done to the forest is insignificant.

C.—Protection Against Birds.

I.—Grouse. The grouse bite-off buds and cotyledons, and eat the fruit of certain tree species (buds of birch, maple, cottonwood; seeds of red cedar, beech, witch hazel, calmia and rhododendron). On the whole the damage done by grouse is inconspicuous.

II.—Wild Turkey. The turkey is useful by eating some noxious insects and by scratching the leaves, thus burying certain tree seeds. At Biltmore, however, on Ducker Mountains, plantations of scarlet oak acorns have been practically destroyed by the turkey. In forest nurseries, as well, the turkey is apt to do considerable harm during the winter.

III.—Pigeons and Doves. Pigeons live during spring and winter on coniferous seeds, beech nuts, buds and cotyledons.

Remedies in nurseries are lath or wire screens or coverings of thorny branches. Pigeons may be shot at anise licks.

IV.—Crows and Bluejays. These birds live on large seeds (acorns, beech nuts, chestnuts) and are especially dangerous in nurseries. They plunder the nests of useful birds. On the other hand, they may assist the forester in destroying mice and noxious insects; they underplant whole forests with acorns, beech nuts, hickory nuts and chestnuts.

V.—Finches and Cross-bills. The damage done consists in the destruction of seed plantations of conifers made in nurseries or in the open. It occurs during the spring migration of the birds when they appear in large swarms.

The cotyledons are bitten off and eaten as well as the seeds. Some cross-bills split the scales of coniferous cones into two, withdrawing the seed from underneath the scales.

Protective measures are:

Screens of wire or lath over nursery beds. The mesh must be fine, and the distance between the lath must not exceed ¾ inch.

Shooting some birds, keeping the balance scared off.

Coating the seeds in red lead (very efficient), one pound of red lead being sufficient to cover seven pounds of coniferous seeds.

Shortening the period of exposure by planting the seeds in late spring after three to eight days mulching.

VI.—Woodpeckers. Woodpeckers withdraw the larvæ of wood boring insects from their mines with the help of a long, thin tongue. They withdraw useful as well as harmful insects. They do damage by opening cones and by eating the seeds thereof.

The damage done by picking holes into the cambium layers of certain trees is small. The holes made in sound yellow poplars rather denote a high quality than the presence of defective timber. The holes made in oak and chestnuts are usually made in rotten or decaying wood, or in wood of no commercial value.

There exist four theories attempting to explain the curious girdles of holes made by the woodpecker.

a.—Incubator Theory.

Holes are picked to invite the ovipositing of insects in such holes.

b.—Napkin Theory.

The woodpecker cleans its beak from particles of rosin.

c.—Calendar Theory.

Due to observation that woodpecker returns at regular intervals to same tree.

d.—Sap-sucking Theory.

Par. 5. Protection Against Insects.

A. General Remarks.

I. Insects are the most serious animal enemies of the forest. More than that, they are the worst enemies of the forest within organic nature.

But in a certain sense, many insects seemingly injurious, are in fact beneficial, since they form one of the means by which nature selects the fittest individuals for the propagation of our trees.

II. Almost all of the orders of insects contain families, some or all the members of which are directly beneficial. These beneficial forms are usually zoophagous, and may be—

a. Predaceous insects feeding on eggs, larvæ, pupæ, or imagines of injurious species, notably—

Order Coleoptera: Families *Coccinellidæ, Cicindelidæ, Carabidæ, Elateridæ, Cleridæ, Trogositidæ, Colydiidæ*
Order Diptera. Families *Asilidæ, Syrphidæ.*
Order Hymenoptera: Superfamily *Formicoidea.*
Order Hemiptera: Family *Reduviidæ.*
Order Orthoptera: Family *Mantidæ.*
Many *Neuropteroid* insects.*

b. Parasitic insects, ovipositing on or in the bodies of injurious species. The more important are—

Order Diptera: Family *Tachinidæ.*
Order Hymenoptera: Superfamilies *Ichneumonoidea, Proctotrypoidea, Chalcidoidea*

c. Parasitic insects, paralyzing their prey by stinging, and carrying them into their nests where the eggs of the parasite are deposited.

Order Hymenoptera: Superfamilies *Sphegoidea, Vespoidea.*

Many families are neither injurious nor beneficial, and are therefore of no economic importance. Other groups which may be either injurious or beneficial to man, are not mentioned here, because they bear no direct relation to forest trees. Amongst the phytophagous insects, there are however, very many forms that are injurious to our forests. Those living on tree weeds must, of course, be considered as beneficial; but speaking gen-

---

*The old order Neuroptera, has been divided into several orders in modern systems of classification. The group as a whole is of little economic importance to the forester, and for that reason, the inclusive term, Neuropteroid, is used.

erally, phytophagous insects found in the forests, are more or less injurious. The families which contain most of the injurious species are—

Order COLEOPTERA: Families *Cerambycidæ, Buprestidæ, Elateridæ, Ptinidæ, Scarabaeidæ, Chrysomelidæ, Curculionidæ, Brenthidæ, Scolytidæ.*
Order LEPIDOPTERA: Families *Arctiidæ, Bombycidæ, Cossidæ, Hesperidæ, Liparidæ, Noctuidæ, Papilionidæ, Zygaenidæ.*

Order HYMENOPTERA: Superfamilies *Tenthredinoidea, Cynipoidea.*

Order HEMIPTERA: Families *Coccidæ, Aphididæ, Cicadidæ.*

Order DIPTERA: Families *Cecidomyiidæ, Syrphidæ.*

Order ORTHOPTERA: Families *Locustidæ, Phasmidæ.*

III. Insects are divided into three groups, according to the relation that exists between the younger stages and the adults.

a. The *Ametabola,* which includes a single order, the THYSANEURA, in which the young and adults differ only in size.

b. The *Hemimetabola,* in which are included the ORTHOPTERA, the HEMIPTERA, etc., etc. In this group the young and adults differ not only in size, but in several other characters, and the young become more and more like the adults after each molt.

c. The *Metabola,* in which are included the COLEOPTERA, LEPIDOPTERA, HYMENOPTERA, DIPTERA, etc., etc. In this group, the young and the adults are totally unlike, and before taking the mature form, the larvæ go through a resting stage.

The first stage of the insect is the egg, and after hatching, it arrives at maturity through a series of molts. On hatching, the young of the *Metabola* are called *larvæ* (caterpillars, maggots, grubs); and in the *Ametabola* and *Hemimetabola,* they are called *nymphs.* There are several molts during the larval or nymphal stage, and the period between any two of them is called an *instar.* The quiescent stage during which the larvæ of the *Metabola* change to imagines, is called the *pupa;*

and the mature or reproductive stage of all insects is called the *adult*, or *imago*. The pupa of a butterfly is very often called a *chrysalis*, and the silken sack spun by many insects in which to pupate, is the *cocoon*. Larvæ of DIPTERA and of some other insects, pupate within a tough outer covering commonly supposed to be simply a pupal skin. The true pupa is, however, entirely within it, and the tough outer covering is distinguished by the name *puparium*. After reaching the adult stage, the insect does not become any larger, and does not molt; its only function is to mate, and lay eggs Some species are unable even to feed after becoming adult, and in almost all cases, the larvæ or nymphs are much more voracious than the mature insects. In general, then, the greater part of the insect damage to our forests is done before the insects responsible become mature. The Ambrosia beetles form a notable exception to this rule.

The sum total of the stages of development of an insect is termed a *generation*, and a given species may be *single-brooded, double-brooded, treble-brooded*, etc., according to the number of generations which occur during a single year. Many insects require more than a single year to complete a generation, and are then called *biennial, triennial*, etc A species of the Cicadidæ is known to have a life round of seventeen years.

IV. CLIMATIC AND SEASONAL CONDITIONS AFFECTING INSECT LIFE. In general, the number of species of insect life decreases as altitude or latitude increases, while at the same time, the number of individuals of a species becomes larger The number of generations of a given species is also affected by the climate; for instance, a species which is "double-brooded" in the Middle States, may become "treble-brooded" in the Southern States, and "single-brooded" in Canada.

Insects spend the winter months in a resting or hibernating stage which varies for the different species. That is, a given species may hibernate either in the egg, larval, pupal, or adult stage They are protected against the cold either by their own coverings, or by the hiding places selected by them in the trees, in the bark, in the moss and leaves, in the stumps, or in the ground. Extreme cold is no more likely to injure the insect than it is to kill the tree itself; but sudden changes of temperature and moisture, especially cold wet spells in late spring, or after a premature thaw has drawn the hibernating insects from their winter quarters, may be disastrous to large numbers of certain species, particularly during the molting periods of the larvæ.

V. Insect Plagues. A succession of favorable springs, free from late frosts and wet spells, is apt to result in an anomalous multiplication of a species. Hence, according to European records, insect plagues, like successions of favorable climatic conditions, occur and recur after periodic intervals. The effects of parasitism however, are very likely to be confused with climatic effects in these records, and too much dependance should not be placed on them. These periodic plagues of insects are very likely to occur in spite of all human ingenuity. But experience teaches us that, in the great majority of cases, nature may be trusted to restore the balance that has been so disturbed. An abnormal increase in the numbers of a given species not only is likely to reduce the natural food supply of such a species so that many individuals will die of starvation, but the parasitic and predaceous enemies of the species also enormously increase in numbers, being encouraged to do so by the abundance of the food on which they exist, and by the ease with which it may be obtained. For the same reason, bacterial and fungous diseases have a better opportunity to spread from one individual to another. The years following an insect plague are, therefore, very likely to be exceptionally free from the particular species involved. Consequently, a plague of this sort usually lasts for but one or two years, although in exceptional cases it may last for three or four years. In the forest, an insect plague, in which several species are often involved, is likely to follow in the wake of a destructive fire or storm, or of an attack by fungi. In any case where such a plague has swept through the forest the dead trees should be marketed immediately if the conditions are at all favorable. Otherwise the resulting loss will be much more serious.

The amount of damage done by a serious outbreak of insects in a forest will depend very largely on the nature of the species involved. If the species is "monophagous," that is, dependent for its food supply only on a single species of tree, it is likely to cause serious losses only in localities where pure stands of the particular tree occur, or, at least, where the trees of that species are not so scattered through the forest as to make it difficult for the adult females of the injurious insect to find a suitable place for oviposition. Polyphagous insects, on the other hand, affect many host trees; and while they are likely to distribute their injuries, so that their effect on the forest is less noticeable, still the ultimate losses extending over a period of years, may be very great. A species imported accidentally from one country to another, is much more likely than a native species to cause serious losses, because of the absence of native parasites and other enemies which serve to keep it in check in its original habitat. The extensive ravages of the Gipsy Moth in Massachusetts, which have lasted over a long period of years, is without precedent in European countries, although the species has been abundant over a large part of the continent of Europe, probably for several centuries.

It may be that insect plagues play a role in the natural change of species of plants coinciding with geological periods, but the question is one of speculation, not demonstration.

VI. Species of Trees Affected. There are no species which are not liable to insect attack, but some are much less susceptible than others. Conifers have, on the whole, less recuperative powers than broad-leaved species, and consequently succumb much more readily to insect attacks. In this country, the spruces and pines, wherever occurring in pure and even-aged forests, are the species which suffer most.

VII. Condition of Trees Affected. We may divide injurious insects into three classes according to the condition of the trees attacked.

a. Certain species, notable those that feed on leaves and pith, usually prefer healthy to diseased plants. They may either kill the tree outright or weaken it to such an extent that conditions are made favorable for the attacks of—

b. species which generally prefer unhealthy trees. Ordinarily these species never attack healthy plants, but in years of plagues they may be forced to do so. Thus in years of extreme abundance, millions of bark-beetles may be drowned in the resin of healthy pines before the trees are weakened to an extent sufficient to allow subsequent millions to propagate the species.

c. Certain other species only attack the trees after they have been killed. Dead timber, either standing or on the ground, should be marketed as soon as possible as a precaution against damage. Decaying logs and stumps are always found infested with numerous species of insects which cannot be classed as injurious since they merely hasten the process of decay. Those insects of this class which are injurious are of less importance to the forester than to the purchaser of his product. Some of them cause serious losses in lumber yards, ship yards, bark sheds, factories, etc.

Insects of classes "a" and "b" above are sometimes called "parasitic" because they attack living plants, as distinguished from those of class "c," which feed only on dead timber, and are called "saprophytic." The term "parasite," however, is commonly used in Entomology to denote a species of insect which has another species for its host, and the student should be careful in his reading to distinguish between the broader and narrower uses of the term.

VIII. Part of Tree Attacked. No part of the tree is entirely free from insect injury. According to species, insects may feed upon the buds (caterpillar causing the fork in the ash), the leaves (elm leaf-beetle), the fruit (chestnut and acorn weevils), the pith (locust shoot-borer), the cambium (larvæ of the so-called bark-beetles), the heart-wood (chestnut borers), the sap-wood (many of the longicorn borers), the roots (larvæ of May-beetles), and the bark (notably tan-bark).

IX. Degree of Damage. According to the amount of damage done, insects may be classed as *a*, Damaging insects; *b*, Destructive insects, and *c*, Pernicious insects. Insects are called *physiologically obnoxious* if they check the growth or propagation of plants, and *technically obnoxious* if they destroy or reduce the technical value without checking the growth The Hemlock bark-maggot furnishes a good example of the last named class

---

B. REMEDIES AND PREVENTIVES IN GENERAL AGAINST INSECT INJURY.

I. Select the proper species for reproduction on a given soil.

II. Encourage mixed forests.

III. Avoid large continuous clearings.

IV. Use the ranger staff in controlling the insects.

V. Remove the weak trees, and strengthen the remaining individuals by means of thinnings.

VI. Protect and improve the productiveness of the soil.

VII. Protect the forest from damage by storm, sleet, or fire in the wake of which insect plagues frequently follow.

VIII. Remove or poison stumps if they are found to form the incubators or food-objects of a noxious insect during one of its stages.

IX. Peel off the bark where logs are left on the ground for any considerable length of time.

X. Encourage hog pastures in the case of certain species of insects. With other species, steep walled ditches may prevent the enemy from spreading in nurseries and plantations.

XI. Protect the insectivorous animals, notably:—

a. Bats, moles, weasels, foxes, etc.
b. Woodpeckers, tits, owls, etc.
c. Amphibia.
d. Spiders.
e. Centipedes, millipedes, etc.

XII. Collect and destroy the insect in that stage which best allows remedial measures to be taken.

a. Eggs may be tarred or covered with creosote when they are placed in masses in conspicuous positions.

b. Larvæ may be destroyed by spraying the food plant with arsenicals or other stomach poisons, or the insects themselves with kerosene or other contact poisons; by trapping them on or below bands of burlap or tree tanglefoot; by the use of trap trees; or by burning their winter quarters or the object (bark) forming their abode.

c. Pupæ may sometimes be collected and burned, particularly when the insect hibernates in this stage.

d. Adults may be beaten off the bushes during the early morning; may be collected during the hot hours of the day in artificial hiding places; or may be caught by means of pit-falls, tanglefoot or burlap rings, trap trees, or electric lights.

The selection of a method of treatment depends not only upon the species of insect concerned, but upon many factors entering into the local conditions. In general, prevention is better than the application of a remedy. This is particularly true in the present status of American forest conditions; and the use of insecticides is only profitable in rare instances. *Indeed in America the forester will frequently be prevented from adopting any measures whatever, remedial or preventive, because the cost will exceed the value of the benefit to be derived.* But in no case should a remedy be attempted by one who is not fully informed as to the life history and food-habits of the insect enemy, and with the remedy to be used. In either event more damage than benefit may result. For instance, trap-trees may often be successfully used against certain insect pests, but unless destroyed at the proper time, just before the emergence of the adults, the numbers of the enemy will be increased rather than diminished. The advice of a competent Forest Entomologist should be obtained wherever possible.

C. INSECT ANATOMY.

I. The body of an adult insect is divided into three regions.

a. The head consists of a single segment, and bears exteriorly a pair of *antennæ*, a pair of *compound eyes*, the *ocelli*, which vary in number and are often absent, and the *mouth parts*, consisting of the *labrum*, two *mandibles*, two *maxillæ*, and the *labium*. Maxillary and labial *palpi* are also present, sometimes so modified however as to be not easily recognizable. The difference between "biting" and "sucking" mouth parts is important both in classification and as regards methods of treatment.

b. The thorax consists of three segments, the *prothorax*, the *mesothorax*, and the *metathorax*. Each segment bears a pair of *legs*, and the mesothorax and metathorax normally bear the *fore* and *hind wings*. The legs are also segmented, the joints bearing the following names: The segment attached to the thorax is called the *coxa*, then come in order the *trochanter* (sometimes made up of two short segments), the *femur*, the *tibia*, and lastly the *tarsus* made up of several segments on the last of which are borne the claws. The wings are composed of two membranes held together by supporting rods called *veins*, or *nerves*, and are sometimes covered with *hairs* or *scales*. In the case of the COLEOPTERA, the fore wings (*Elytra*) are hard and leathery, and the veins are absent.

c. The abdomen consists of several segments, some or all with *stigmata* or breathing pores. The external reproductive organs are usually borne on the last or anal segment of the abdomen. In certain species an *ovipositor* (laying-tube), or a saw-like instrument assists the female in oviposition.

II. THE LARVA. In the larvæ of the *Metabola*, as in the adult insect, the first segment is the head, the next three make up the thorax, and the remainder of the body is called the abdomen; but the three regions are not so distinct as is the case with the imago. The mouth parts are almost always for "biting," and have the same names as in the imago. The spinnarets of certain caterpillars, situated in the mouth, are the apertures of long glands, which traverse the entire body. If present, the antennæ are rudimentary. If legs are present, there are always three pairs, situated on the ventral side of the thoracic segments. Sometimes there are also legs on some of the abdominal segments, but these are more properly called *pro-legs*, and are not segmented.

III. THE NYMPH. In the Ametabola and the Hemimetabola, the anatomy of the younger stages is similar to that of the imago.

IV. THE PUPA. The pupa is called *carved* or *masked*, according to the ease with which legs, antennæ, mouth parts, etc., can be distinguished through the *pupa case*. The outer web of silk spun for protection by many LEPIDOPTERA and HYMENOPTERA is called the *cocoon*.

V. THE EGG. Insect eggs vary greatly in form. They may be cup-shaped or kidney-shaped, crater-formed or mucronate, round, oval, or canoe-shaped. Very rarely they are stalked.

VI. INTERNAL ANATOMY. In an insect, this consists of *a*, the Endoskeleton; *b*, Musculature; *c*, the Digestive System; (œsophagus, crop, proventriculus, stomach, hind-gut, salivary and other glands, Malpighian tubes, etc.); *d*, the Nervous System, (brain, subœsophageal ganglion, thoracic and abdominal ganglia, nerve cord, motor and sensory nerves); *e*, the Circulatory System, (the heart and blood); *f*, the Respiratory System, (stigmata and trachæ or trachæal-gills); and *g*, the Reproductive Organs, (ovaries, ovarian tubes, and oviduct in the female; spermaries and vasa deferentia in the male).

INSECT FAMILIES ARRANGED ACCORDING TO FOOD OBJECTS IN THE FOREST.

		Compare Page of Ent. Bul. No. 48
	I. Infesting the Cambial Bark.	
Bark Beetles	Scolytidæ (excepting Platypini, larvæ and adults)...	9
Flat and round headed borers:	Buprestidæ, Cerambycidæ (mines often extending into wood prior to pupation)...	10
Bark weevils:	Curculionidæ ...	10
Powder post beetles:	Ptinidæ, (in peeled tan bark)...	11
	II. Infesting the Wood.	
Ambrosia or timber beetles:	Scolytidæ (larvæ and adults)...	10
Wood-boring caterpillars:	Sesiidæ ...	10
True woodboring beetle-grubs:	Lymexilonidæ, Brenthidæ...	10
Bark and wood boring grubs:	Curculionidæ, Cerambycidæ, Buprestidæ...	10
Carpenter worms:	Cossidæ ...	11
Horn tails:	Siricidæ ...	11
Powder post beetles:	Lyctidæ, Ptinidæ, Bostrichidæ (dead wood only)...	11
	III. Injuring Leaves or Needles.	
True Caterpillars and measuring worms:	Lepidoptera (practically all families of the order) ..	11
False caterpillars	Tenthredinidæ ...	12
Leaf beetles:	Chrysomelidæ ...	12
Gall insects:	Cynipidæ, Cecidomyiidæ, Aphididæ ...	12
Plant lice:	Aphididæ, Psyllidæ...	12
Scale insects:	Coccidæ ...	12
	IV. Infesting Twigs.	
Twig mining beetles:	Scolytidæ, Buprestidæ, Cerambycidæ...	12
Twig weevils:	Curculionidæ ...	13
Twig caterpillars:	Tineidæ, Tortricidæ...	13
Scale insects:	Coccidæ ...	13
Plant lice:	Aphididæ ...	13
Gall insects:	Cecidomyiidæ and Cynipidæ ...	13
Cicadas:	Cicadidæ ...	13
	V. Infesting Young Seedlings in Nurseries.	
Cutworms:	Noctuidæ ...	
Junebugs:	Scarabæidæ ...	

Means of Protection

I. PROTECTION AGAINST INSECTS INFESTING THE CAMBIAL BARK OF THE TRUNK.

A. Against Scolytidæ (Bark Beetles).

(1) Conduct the logging operations at that season of the year at which the logs are apt to become infested; and after infection, remove the bark, entirely or partially; or move the logs rapidly to water or mill. In other cases, conduct logging at that season at which the debris left are not apt to form incubators for Scolytidæ, or else long before swarming (e. g., cut pine at Biltmore in early winter, to avoid *Dendroctonus frontalis*). Compare Agric Year Book, 1902, p. 275 for *D. frontalis* and p. 281 for *D. ponderosæ*.

(2) Girdle, peel, lodge, fall or blaze trap trees of inviting diameter, shape and position prior to the time of the swarming of the Scolytidæ Compare Agric. Year Book, 1902, p. 269. Trap trees might be prepared in the district to be logged next. Try to destroy the trapped Scolytidæ without injury to the Cleridæ and their allies.

(3) Remove or burn logging debris; or swamp the tree tops left, thus creating unfavorable conditions of moisture. Sometimes it is possible to use the debris as traps Compare, however, Entom Bul. No 21, p. 23, for advice to leave the debris, so as to divert predatory Scolytidæ from sound trees to debris.

(4) Leave all trees (also trap trees) in the woods which prove to be incubators for Ichneumonidæ, Braconidæ, Chalcididæ. Remove the outer bark so as to assist ovipositing Ichneumons in reaching their prey. Introduce and breed parasites. (Bul. West Va. Agr. Station, p 326.)

(5) Counteract reckless deadening by farmers engaged in clearing their fields

(6) Adopt proper diameter limit in logging where a Scolytid attacks only trees of certain diameter classes. Remember, e. g, that the spruce having under 10'' d.b.h is safe from *D piceaperda*

(7) Begin logging in districts recently damaged by fire, storm, sleet.

(8) Remove even worthless trees, if they are apt to act as incubators. Keep in mind, on the other hand, that trees with dead cambium are not attacked by cambium boring Scolytidæ.

(9) Have at hand, ready for use, permanent means of transportation so as to be able to operate when and where you ought to operate; particularly, *when and where timber begins to die.*

(10) Conduct thinnings in a manner and at a time counteracting infection by Scolytidæ Remove dying and injured (by lightning) trees, also trees weakened in vigor.

(11) Watch for spider webs showing saw dust; for drops of rosin (pitch tubes) appearing on the bark, for a local increase of woodpeckers indicating an increase of food material; for a slight change in the tint of the pine-crowns.

(12) Apply sprays or washes, twice or thrice per season, to particularly valuable trees (Forest Bul. No. 22, p. 56), e. g., lime and Paris green, mixed to a mass of light green color, or soft soap, adding enough washing soda and water to reduce the mixture to the consistency of a thick paint; or a thick wash of soap, Paris green and plaster of Paris; or a mixture of one pint of carbolic acid, one gallon of soft soap and eight gallons of soft water Arsenate of lead may be used instead of Paris green, and has a greater insecticidal value.

B. Against Buprestidæ and Cerambycidæ (Flat-headed and Round-headed Borers).

(1) Prepare trap trees, or use trees accidentally injured or weakened as such.

(2) Remove, peel, burn or immerse in water, trees in weakened condition. Begin logging in districts containing such trees (e. g., blowdowns, burns).

(3) Prevent ground fires which weaken the trees, burst their bark and render them liable to successful attacks by Buprestids and Cerambycids Try to retain the fertility of the soil

(4) Protect insectivorous animals (compare Bureau of Entomology Bulletin No. 28, p 23)

(5) Prevent trees left in the course of logging from being recklessly injured by axe, by felled trees striking them, etc

(6) Where you remove a portion only of the trees standing in the woods, log in winter (not in spring and summer).

C. Against Curculionidæ ("Bark Weevils").

(1) Remove the trees which appear injured by axe, lightning, storm, sleet or the fall of a neighbor.

(2) Prepare trap trees, and destroy the brood of Curculionids developing therein in due season.

D. Against Ptinidæ.

Mind that the bark is safe from powderpost beetles for two years, and do not store any tan bark for more than two years

II. PROTECTION AGAINST INSECTS BORING IN WOOD AND TIMBER.

A. Against Scolytidæ ("Ambrosia Beetles").

(1) Remove infested trees or logs prior to swarming.

(2) Cut low stumps, or poison or char the stumps.

(3) Remove bark from all logs liable to be affected or throw the logs into water. Do not leave in the woods any summer-felled logs.

(4) Log all blow-downs and brules as rapidly as possible.

(5) Have all parts of the woods continuously accessible to logging, by establishing permanent means of transportation.

(6) Prevent ruthless deadening by farmers. Girdle cypress, oak and ash—preparatory to driving or rafting—after the swarming season of the Scolytids.

(7) In orchards or gardens, coat the treetrunks with dendrolene; spray them with kerosene; plug the holes bored, leave a nail therein, or use a deterrent wash (compare Bureau of Forestry Bulletin No. 46, p. 66).

(8) Do not leave any logs in the woods or in the log yard for any length of time. In case of logging in spring and summer, peel off the bark.

B Against Lymexylonidæ and Brenthidæ.

(1) Reproduce the chestnut from seedlings, not from sprouts Remove dead limbs quickly, and cover the scar with tar.

(2) Prevent the bark of the chestnut from being injured and opened by fires, by the fall of neighboring trees, by axe wounds, etc.

On the other hand, scarify a number of trees to be cut and removed in the course of your operations in the near future. Strip off the bark in narrow bands, or blaze and hack through it as high as the axe will reach. Do this towards the time when the chestnut begins to bloom. The swarming insect deposits her eggs into the scars made, and all trees thus treated act as trap trees.

(3) Do not leave any cord wood or any logs of chestnut in the forest after June 15, so as to remove insects contained therein before hatching.

(4) Keep the forest dense, dark, moist, cool.

C. Against Cerambycidæ (Round-headed Borers).

(1) Cut in summer and peel the bark of the logs cut; or remove a horizontal strip of bark along and on top of the log. The moisture gathering in the gutter thus made prevents the grubs from developing.

(2) Log rapidly after heavy conflagrations, blowdowns or plagues of bark beetles. Readiness to remove dead timber minimizes the damage by Cerambycids If removal is impossible, throw the logs into water, char or peel them.

(3) For shade trees, prevent oviposition by a wash consisting of soap and carbolic acid (compare Report N. Y. Forest, Fish and Game Commission, Vol. IV, p. 21). The borer-holes might be stopped with putty after inserting a little carbon bisulphide (explosive).

D. Against Lyctidæ, Ptinidæ, Bostrichidæ (Powderpost Beetles).

(1) Use heartwood sticks for sticking in lumber piles

(2) Do not dead pile

(3) Spray piles with naphtaline or creoline-Pearson three times, per season.

(4) Impregnate all sapwood before using it.

(5) Keep an eye on all parts of the yard continuously.

(6) Infested pieces of timber should be thoroughly steamed, or impregnated, or liberally treated with gasoline, kerosene, creoline, or kept submerged for a number of weeks (compare Bureau of Entomology, Circular No. 55)

III. PROTECTION AGAINST INSECTS INJURIOUS TO LEAVES, NEEDLES AND BUDS.

A Against Lepidopterous Caterpillars.

(1) Remove—possibly by fire—leaf mould, mosses, brush found at bases of trees where such material forms the winter quarters for the insect.

(2) Apply to the trees bands of burlap, 10″ wide (compare Farmers' Bulletin No. 99, p. 20), or bands of "Tree Tanglefoot", in the latter case either after the removal of the ross on the tree, or on a sheet of oiled paper fastened round the tree. Usually, heavy thinnings precede the application.

(3) Burn the webs of web worms.

(4) Moisten egg heaps with creosote oil (e g., for tussock moth). Use a steel brush to destroy the eggs by rubbing

(5) Spray with washes, remembering, that the underside of the leaves must be sprayed and that the job is well done only when the tree drips. A common wash consists of one pound of Paris green and one pound of quick lime dissolved in 150 gallons of water. An excellent wash is made from arsenate of lime which adheres long, shows its presence by its white color and is harmless to the leaves. See for recipe, also for description of power-spray, New York Forest, Fish and Game Commission, IV. report, p. 10.

(6) Protect insectivorous birds, snakes, lizards, toads

(7) Confine collected caterpillars as closely together as possible, so as to breed deadly diseases amongst them (e. g., Empusa), or so as to invite counter-plagues (*Microgaster, Pimpla, etc.*)

(8) Catch the swarming moths by exhaust fans placed near strong electric lights.

(9) Allow of hog pasture.

B. Against Tenthredinidæ (Nematus), Aphididæ, Coccidæ, Psyllidæ.

(1) Use of soap wash, prepared by dissolving soap in boiling water, adding kerosene (New York Forest, Fish and Game Commission, IV. report, p. 31), or arsenical insecticides, caustic washes, etc., (for which compare Bureau of Entomology, Bul. No. 7, pp. 33, 37, 45, 51).

(2) Protect insectivorous animals.

(3) Destroy infested plants or, in the case of *Nematus erichsonii*, infested woodlands.

IV. PROTECTION AGAINST INSECTS INFESTING BRANCHES, TWIGS, SHOOTS.

A. Against Scolytidæ.

(1) Collect and burn affected shoots before the larvæ begin to pupate therein.

(2) Use logging debris as traps.

(3) Burn logging debris, or swamp the crowns of felled trees.

B. Against Curculionidæ (Twig Weevils).

(1) Avoid logging and thinning of pinewoods near young pines in the seedling or in the sapling stage.

(2) Remove the top shoots of white pine attacked by *Pissodes strobi*, and keep them in a barrel covered with netting, in the nursery, so as to kill the weevil without destroying its parasites.

(3) Remove, char, peel or poison fresh pine stumps.

(4) Apply to the terminal shoots of white pine, during April or May, a spray consisting of fish oil soap, Paris green and carbolic acid diluted in water (Bureau of Forestry, Bul. No. 22, p. 59).

(5) Use trap trees for oviposition, consisting of fresh-cut pine billets buried obliquely with one end protruding above ground. Burn these traps after the eggs have hatched.

(6) Collect the adults underneath large pieces of fresh pine bark placed on the ground. The adults spend the hot hours of the day underneath the bark attracted by the smell of rosin.

C. Against Cerambycidæ.

(1) Collect limbs broken off by wind and infested by *Elaphidion* (Oak pruner).

(2) Cut off shoots or saplings affected by larvæ.

D. Against Tineidæ and Tortricidæ.

(1) Remove infested shoots.

(2) Apply insecticides.

E. Against Cicadidæ.

(1) Collect larvæ.

(2) Protect crows and owls.

V. PROTECTION AGAINST INSECTS AFFECTING SEEDLINGS IN NURSERIES.

A. Against Curculionidæ.

(1) Do not leave any pine stumps in or near nurseries.

(2) Raise healthy transplants, on well-manured soil.

(3) Collect adults under bark traps, and collect larvæ on billets buried obliquely.

B. Against Scarabæidæ (June Bugs).

(1) Collect adults in early morning from bushes

(2) Cultivate four or five times that section of the nursery which is lying fallow.

(3) Protect insectivorous birds.

(4) Trap the larvæ beneath reversed sods of grass.

(5) Separate the beds by deep trenches.

(6) Irrigate freely—if possible, raising the water in the trenches from time to time to the level of the beds.

(7) Cultivate the beds heavily and frequently, particularly during the winter months.

C. Against Noctuidæ (Cut Worms).

(1) Catch adults at night with sugared apples.

(2) Poison caterpillars with cabbage sprinkled with arsenic and laid along the nursery beds.

(3) Irritate caterpillars by continuous cultivation of soil.

D. Against Cicadidæ.

Do not keep any broad-leaved trees or bushes in or near the nursery on which the eggs might be deposited. Injection of bisulphide of carbon into soil is recommended by Bureau of Entomology, Bul. No. 14, p. 111.

E. Against Gryllidæ (Crickets)

(1) Protect moles, crows, etc.

(2) Keep deep trenches between the beds, and use short beds.

(3) Insert earthenware pots at the intersection of trenches.

(4) Propagate a fungus disease (Empusa Grylli) for which see Bureau of Entomology, Bull. No. 38, p. 53.

(5) Plow the beds deeply before using them.

VI. PROTECTION AGAINST INSECTS INFESTING FRUITS OR SEEDS, I. E., AGAINST CURCULIONIDÆ, TORTRICIDÆ, PHYCITIDÆ.

(1) When wintering chestnuts or acorns, store them in the natural way, not allowing the seeds to become dry. See lectures on Sylviculture.

(2) Plant seeds as soon as possible after collecting.

The following table shows the distinguishing features of the six principal orders of insects, the first eight divisions referring to the adults

ORDER	METAMORPHOSIS	FRONT WINGS	HIND WINGS	PROTHORAX	MOUTH PARTS	ANTENNÆ	TARSUS	OCELLI	EXOSKELETON	LARVA	PUPA
Coleoptera (beetles) (weevils)	Complete	Horny	Membraneous, folded crosswise and lengthwise.	Free	For biting	Comparatively few segments	2 to 5 segments	None	Very hard	Horny head, footless or six-footed.	Carved
Lepidoptera (moths and butterflies)	Complete	Front and hind wings membraneous, with many veins, and covered with colored scales.		Not free	For sucking, proboscis rolled spirally	Usually a great many segments	5 segments	None or 2	Soft	Head distinct, 10, 14, or 16 footed.	Masked, usually within cocoon.
Hymenoptera (ants, wasps, bees, sawflies,) etc.	Complete	Front and hind wings membraneous, with few veins and cross-veins, hind pair smaller than front		Not free	For biting, licking or, sucking	Thread-like, Variable	4 or 5 segments	Usually 3	Medium	6, 8, 18, or 22 feet, or footless	Carved, often within cocoon.
Diptera (flies, mosquitoes, etc.)	Complete	Membraneous with very few veins	Rudimentary, appearing as balancers (halteres)	Not free	For sucking and piercing (proboscis stiff)	3, 5, or more segments	5 segments	2 or 3	Medium	Footless, head sometimes very inconspicuous.	Carved within puparium
Hemiptera (bugs, lice, scale insects, etc.)	In-complete	First half leathery, second half membraneous. Often wingless.	Membraneous if (present)	Free	For sucking and piercing (proboscis jointed laid against breast)	Variable	2 or 3 segments	None or 2	Variable	Resembles the imago	None
Orthoptera (grasshoppers, crickets, etc)	In-complete	Leathery, but veins are distinct.	Membraneous, many veined, folded fan-like	Not free	For biting	Variable	2 to 5 segments	3	Hard	Resembles the imago	None

THE MINES OF INSECTS. With the exception of the *Scolytidæ*, mines and galleries of insects in cambium and wood are made by the larvae. Larval mines usually increase in diameter, the size of the gallery corresponding to the increasing size of the larva. The mines made by the adults of the *Scolytidæ* are characterized by the uniformity of their diameter.

REFERENCE LIST

COMPILED BY F. D. COUDEN AND C. A. SCHENCK

The following pages will refer the student to publications, most of which should be in the library of the up-to-date forester, where accounts, more or less complete, of certain species of insects injurious to forest and shade trees may be found. The list is by no means complete, and it is very likely that a few even of the important species have been omitted. The study of Forest Entomology is still in its infancy; but the literature, while not yet voluminous, is so scattered that it would not be profitable for the present purpose to go through it with a fine-toothed comb. A great many errors will undoubtedly be noticed by Entomologists, particularly as to *synonymy;* but it is hoped, nevertheless, that the list will be of some value to the students of Forestry for whom it is designed.

The arrangement is faulty in that many polyphagous species of insects are not listed under all of their host trees. ***Porthetria dispar***, for instance, is listed only under *Quercus*, whereas the caterpillars of the Gipsy Moth feed indiscriminately on the foilage of almost any tree within their range. The use of the "index," however, will enable the student to find the references to any insect listed, without regard to the host under which the reference is given.

Here follow the complete titles of all the publications used in the preparation of the list. The abbreviations used in the list proper are printed here in Black-Faced Type, and are followed by the titles, names of authors' and years of publication.

UNITED STATES PUBLICATIONS

5th Rept. Ent. Com. U. S. Fifth Report of the United States Entomological Commission. Insects injurious to forest and shade trees. By A. S. Packard. 1890.

Ag. Yr. Bk. for 1895 U. S.—Yearbook of the United States Department of Agriculture for 1895. The Shade Tree insect problem in the eastern United States. By L. O. Howard. pp. 361-384. 1896.

Ag. Yr. Bk. for 1902 U. S.—Yearbook of the United States Department of Agriculture for 1902. Some of the principal insect enemies of coniferous forests in the United States. By A. D. Hopkins. pp. 265-282. 1903.

Ag. Yr. Bk. for 1903 U. S.—Yearbook of the United States Department of Agriculture for 1903. Insects injurious to hardwood forest trees. By A. D. Hopkins. pp. 313-328. 1904.

Ag. Yr. Bk. for 1904 U. S.—Yearbook of the United States Department of Agriculture for 1904. Insect injuries to forest products. By A. D. Hopkins. pp. 381-398. The nut weevils. By F. H. Chittenden. pp. 299-310. 1905.

Ag. Yr. Bk. for 1905 U. S.—Yearbook of the United States Department of Agriculture for 1905. Insect enemies of forest reproduction. By A. D. Hopkins. pp. i-iii and 249-256. 1906.

Ag. Yr. Bk. for 1907 U. S.—Yearbook of the United States Department of Agriculture for 1907. Notable depredations by forest insects. By A. D. Hopkins. pp. i-iii and 149-164. 1908.

Bulletins of the Bureau (Formerly Division) of Entomology, United States Department of Agriculture.

Ent. Bul. No. 7 U. S.—Some miscellaneous results of the work of the Division of Entomology. The ambrosia beetles of the United States. By H. G. Hubbard. pp. 9-30. Insect injuries to chestnut and pine trees in Virginia and neighboring states. By F. H. Chittenden. pp. 67-75. 1897.

Ent. Bul. No. 14 U. S.—The Periodical Cicada. By C. L. Marlatt. 1898.

Ent. Bul. No. 21 U. S.—Preliminary report on the insect enemies of forests in the Northwest. By A. D. Hopkins. 1899.

Ent. Bul. No. 28 U. S.—Insect enemies of the spruce in the Northwest. By A. D. Hopkins. 1901.

Ent. Bul. No. 32 U. S.—Insect enemies of pine in the Black Hills. By A. D. Hopkins. 1902.

Ent. Bul. No. 37 U. S.—Proceedings of the fourteenth annual meeting of the Association of Economic Entomologists. On the study of forest entomology in America. By A. D. Hopkins. pp. 5-32. 1902.

Ent. Bul. No. 38 U. S.—Some miscellaneous results of the work of the Division of Entomology. Notes on the Rhinocerus Beetle. By F. H. Chittenden. pp. 28-32. 1902.

Ent. Bul. No. 48 U. S.—Catalogue of exhibits of insect enemies of forest products at the Louisiana Purchase Exposition, St. Louis, Mo., 1904. By A. D. Hopkins. 1904.

Ent. Bul. No. 53 U. S.—Catalogue of the exhibit of Economic Entomology at the Lewis and Clrak Centennial Exposition, Portland, Oregon, 1905. By Rolla P. Currie. 1904.

Ent. Bul. No. 56 U. S.—The Black Hills Beetle. By A. D. Hopkins. 1905.

Ent. Bul. No. 58 U. S.—Some insects injurious to forests. Parts I, II, and III. By A. D. Hopkins and J. L. Webb. 1906-07.

Ent. Bul. No. 71 U. S.—The Periodical Cicada. By C. L. Martlatt. 1907.

Circulars of the Bureau (Formerly Division) of Entomology of the United States Department of Agriculture.

Ent. Cir. No. 24 U. S.—The Two-lined Chestnut Borer. By F. H. Chittenden. 1897.

Ent. Cir. No. 29 U. S.—The Fruit-tree Bark-beetle. By F. H. Chittenden. 1898.

Ent. Cir. No. 55 U. S.—Powder-post injury to seasoned wood products. By F. H Chittenden. 1903

Ent. Cir. No. 82 U. S.—Pinhole injury to girdled cypress in the South Atlantic and Gulf States. By A. D. Hopkins. 1907.

Ent. Cir. No. 83 U. S.—The Locust Borer, and methods for its control. By A. D. Hopkins. 1907.

Ent. Cir. No. 90 U. S.—The White-pine Weevil. By A D. Hopkins. 1907.

Ent. Cir. No. 96 U. S.—The Catalpa Sphinx. By L. O. Howard and F. H. Chittenden. 1907.

Ent. Cir. No. 97 U. S.—The Bagworm. By L. O. Howard and F. H Chittenden. 1908.

Bulletins of the Forest Service (Formerly Bureau of Forestry) of the United States Department of Agriculture.

For. Bul. No. 22 U. S.—The White Pine. Insect enemies of———. By F. H. Chittenden. pp. 55-61. 1899.

For. Bul. No. 31 U. S.—The Western Hemlock. Insects of the———. By A. D. Hopkins. pp. 16-21. 1902.

For. Bul. No. 38 U. S.—The Redwood. Insects of the———. By A. D. Hopkins. pp 32-40. 1903.

For. Bul. No. 46 U. S.—The Basket Willow. Insects injurious to———. By F. H. Chittenden. pp. 63-80. 1904.

Other Publications of the United States Department of Agriculture.

Far. Bul. No. 99 U. S.—Farmer's Bulletin No. 99. Three insect enemies of shade trees. By L. O. Howard. 1899.

Far. Bul. No. 264 U. S.—Farmer's Bulletin No. 264. The Brown-tail Moth, and how to control it. By L. O. Howard. 1906.

Far. Bul. No. 265 U. S.—Farmer's Bulletin No. 265. The Gipsy Moth, and how to control it. By L. O. Howard. 1907.

F'ld. Pr'g'm. F'st. S'ce.-April, 1907, U. S.—Field Programme of the Forest Service for April, 1907.

STATE PUBLICATIONS.

New Jersey.

Geol. Rept. for 1899. N. J.—Annual Report of the State Geologist of New Jersey for the year 1899. Part III. Report on Forests. The role of insects in the forest. By J. B. Smith. pp. 205-232. 1899.

New York.

G'de. L'fl't. No. 16 A. M. N. H.—Guide Leaflet No. 16, American Museum of Natural History. The insect galls of the vicinity of New York City. By William Beutenmuller. 1904.

Ex. Sta. Bul. No. 233 Cornell.—Cornell University. Agricultural Experiment Station of the College of Agriculture. Bulletin No. 233. Department of Entomology. Saw-fly leaf-miners on European elms and alders. By M. V. Slingerland. 1905.

Ex. Sta. Bul. No. 234 Cornell.—Cornell University. Agricultural Experiment Station of the College of Agriculture. Bulletin No. 234. Department of Entomology. The Bronze Birch-borer. By M. V. Slingerland. 1906.

For. Rept. No. 4 N. Y.—Fourth annual report of the Commissioners of Fisheries, Game, and Forests of the State of New York. Report for 1898. Insects injurious to maple trees. By E. P. Felt. pp. 367-395. 1899.

For. Rept. No. 7 N. Y.—Seventh annual report of the Forest, Fish, and Game Commission of the State of New York. Report for 1901. Insects affecting forest trees. By E. P. Felt. pp. 479-534. 1902.

St. Mus. Bul. No. 53 N. Y.—New York State Museum Bulletin No. 53. (Entomology 14). 17th Report of the State Entomologist on injurious and other insects of the State of New York. By E. P. Felt. 1901.

St. Mus. Bul. No. 103 N. Y.—New York State Museum Bulletin No. 103. (Entomology 25). The Gipsy and Brown-tail Moths. By E. P. Felt. 1906.

St. Mus. Bul. No. 109 N. Y.—New York State Museum Bulletin No. 109. (Entomology 27). White-marked Tussock-moth and Elm Leaf-beetle. By E. P. Felt. 1907.

St. Mus. Bul. No. 110 N. Y.—New York State Museum Bulletin No. 110. (Entomology 28). 22nd Report of the State Entomologist on injurious and other insects of the state of New York. By E. P. Felt. 1907.

St. Mus. Mem. No. 8 N. Y.—New York State Museum Memoir 8. 2 volumes. Insects affecting park and woodland trees. By E. P. Felt. 1905-06.

OHIO.

Ins. Bul. No. 7 Ohio.—Ohio Department of Agriculture. Division of Nursery and Orchard Inspection. Bulletin No. 7. The insects affecting the black locust and hardy catalpa. By E. C. Cotton. 1905.

PENNSYLVANIA.

For. Rept. 1901-02 Penn.—Statement of work done by the Pennsylvania Department of Forestry during 1901 and 1902. 1902.

WEST VIRGINIA.

Ex. Sta. Bul. No. 35 W. Va.—Bulletin of the West Virginia Agricultural Experiment Station No. 35. Defects in wood caused by insects. By A. D. Hopkins. 1894.

Ex. Sta. Bul. No. 56 W. Va.—Bulletin of the West Virginia Agricultural Experiment Station No. 56. Report on investigations to determine the cause of unhealthy conditions of the spruce and pine from 1880 to 1893. By A. D. Hopkins. 1899.

MISCELLANEOUS PUBLICATIONS.

Comstock's Manual.—Manual for the Study of Insects. By J. H. Comstock. 1895.

Ratzeburg Vol. III.—Die Forst-Insecten, volume III. By J. C. Ratzeburg. Berlin, 1844.

The Forester for 1901.—The Forester. A periodical published by the American Forestry Association at Washington, D. C.

Damage to Pinus strobus by Coleoptera

Family	Genus	Species	Parts Suffering	Literary References: 5th Rept Ent Com U. S.	Ent Bul No. 48 U. S	Ent Bul No. 53 U S	Ent. Bul. No. 7 U S	Ent. Bul. No 32 U. S	For. Bul No 22 U S.	Ag Yr Bk for 1902 U S	For. Rept. No 7 N Y	Ex. Sta. No 35 W. Va.	Ex Sta No. 56 W. Va	St. Mus No. 8 N. Y.	Ent. Cir. No 90 U. S.	Ag Yr.Bk for 1905 U. S.
Cerambycidæ	*Arhopalus*	*fulminans* Fab.	Bole	343	37	95								444		
	Asemum	*mæstum* Hald	Bole	697	35	93							438	661		
	Monohammus	*scutellatus* Say	Bole	696	21, 35	76, 92			57			299[4]		364		
	Rhagium	*lineatum* Oliv	Bole	704	37	96					492			366		
Buprestidæ	*Buprestis*	*aurulenta* Linn.	Bole		39	98										
	Chalcophora	*virginiensis* Dru.	Bole	676	39	98			58				436	653		
Curculionidæ	*Hylobius*	*pales* Hbst.	Bole	724	34	92							441	664		
	Pachylobius	*picivorus* Germ.	Bole	727	34	92										
	Pissodes	*strobi* Peck	Bole	734	34	91			58				441	397	all	252
Scolytidæ	*Crypturgus*	*atomus* Lec	Twigs	826	26	82								359		
	**Dendroctonus*	*frontalis* Zimm.	Bole	722	41, 44	100, 101	73		55	270				342		
	**Dendroctonus*	*terebrans* Oliv	Bole	721							480		394			
	**Dendroctonus*	*valens* Lec.	Bole		19	74		12								
	Dryocœtes	n. sp.			25	81										
	Gnathotrichus	*materiarius* Fitch.	Bole	719	15	70	30		57		495			371		
	Hylastes	*cavernosus* Zimm	Bole										356			
	Hylurgops	*glabratus* Zeff.	Bole										[3]294	665		
	Pityogenes	n. sp.	Twigs		25	80					490					
	Pityophthorus	n sp.	Twigs	715[1]	24	80					492					
	***Platypus*	*compositus* Say	Bole		39											
	Tomicus	*avulsus* Eichh	Bole		41, 44	100							422			
	Tomicus	*cacographus* Lec	Twigs	713					56		485		422	356		
	Tomicus	*calligraphus* Germ.	Bole	711							482		294, 422	345		
	Tomicus	*cœlatus* Eichh		706[2]							488		423	354		
	Tomicus	*pini* Say	Bole & Twigs	713							487		385, 422	351		

[1]As *P. annectens*? [2]As *Xyleborus*. [3]As *H. Pinifex* [4]As "Pine Sawyer" *Also Ag. Yr. Bk for 1907, p. 163. **Also Ent. Cir. No. 82, p. 2.

Damage to Pinus lambertiana by Coleoptera

Family	Genus	Species	Parts Suffering	Literary References						
				Ent. Bul. No. 48 U. S.	Ent. Bul. No. 53 U. S.	Ent. Bul. No. 37 U. S	Ent. Bul. No. 21 U S.	The Forester for 1901	Field Program Forest Service April, 1907	Ag. Yr. Bk. for 1907 U. S.
Curculionidæ	*Pissodes*	?	Bole	22	78	----	----	-----	----------	-----
Scolytidæ	*Carphoborus*	n. sp.	Bole	18	73	----	----	-----	----------	-----
	Dendroctonus	*brevicomis* Lec.	Bole	18	74	----	----	-----	----------	162
	Dendroctonus	*monticolæ* Hopk	Bole	----	----	----	----	-----	21	162
	Dendroctonus	n sp.	Bole	19, 45	74	----	----	-----	----------	-----
	Hylurgops	*subcostulatus* Mann	Bole	19	74	----	----	-----	----------	-----
	Tomicus	*latidens* Lec.	Twigs	17	72	----	----	-----	----------	-----
	Tomicus	*monticola* Hopk	Bole	----	----	21	[1]20	251	----------	-----
	Tomicus	n. sp.	Bole	19	73	----	----	-----	----------	-----

[1]As *Tomicus* sp. (allied to *confusus*).

Damage to Pinus monticola and P. flexilis by Coleoptera

Family	Genus	Species	Parts Suffering	Literary References												
				5th Rept Ent. Com. U. S.	Ent Bul. No. 48 U. S.	Ent Bul No. 53 U. S.	Ent. Bul. No. 37 U. S.	Ent. Bul. No. 32 U. S.	Ent. Bul. No 21 U. S.	For Bul. No. 22 U. S.	For. Rept. No. 7 N. Y.	Ex. Sta No. 35 W. Va.	The Forst'r for 1901	Fld Prg For.Ser. Apr. '07	Ag.Yr.Bk. for 1907 U. S.	St. Mus. No. 8 N. Y.
Cerambycidæ ?[2]	*Monohammus*	*scutellatus* Say	Bole	606	21, 35	76, 92	----	----	----	58	[2]404	300	----	----	----	384
Scolytidæ	*Dendroctonus*	*monticola* Hopk.	Bole	----	42, 45[1]	101	21	----	[1]20	----	----	----	251	21	162	----
	Dendroctonus	n. sp.	Bole	----	19	74	----	----	----	----	----	----	----	----	----	----
	Hylurgops	*subcostulatus* Mann	Bole	----	19	74	----	13	----	----	----	----	----	----	----	----
	Pityogenes	n. sp.	Bole	----	17	72	----	----	----	----	----	----	----	----	----	----
	Pityophthorus	*nitidulus* Mann.	Twigs	----	17	72	----	----	----	----	----	----	----	----	----	----
	Pityophthorus	*puncticollis* Lec.	Bole	----	16	72	----	----	----	----	----	----	----	----	----	----
	Pityophthorus	n. sp.	Bole	----	17	72	----	----	----	----	----	----	----	----	----	----
	Tomicus	n. sp.	Bole	----	18	73	----	----	----	----	----	----	----	----	----	----

[1]As *dendroctonus* n. sp. [2]On *M. Confusor*, a nearly related species.

Damage to Pinus murrayana by Coleoptera

Family	Genus	Species	Parts Suffering	Literary References								
				5th Rept. Ent. Com. U. S.	Ent. Bul. No. 48 U. S.	Ent. Bul No. 53 U. S.	Ent. Bul No 32 U. S.	Ent. Bul. No. 21 U. S.	For. Rept No. 7 N. Y.	F'ld. Pr'g'm F'r'st S'r'ce. Apr., 1907	Ag. Yr. Bk. for 1907 U. S.	St. Mus. Mem. No. 8 N. Y.
Scolytidæ	*Dendroctonus*	*monticolæ* Hopk.	Bole	-----	----	----	----	----	-----	21	162	---------
	Dendroctonus	*valens* Lec.	Bole	-----	19	74	12	----	-----	-------	-----	---------
	Dendroctonus	n. sp	Bole	-----	42, 45	101	----	----	-----	-------	-----	---------
	Hylurgops	*subcostulatus* Mann	Bole	-----	19	74	13	----	-----	-------	-----	---------
	Pityophthorus	n. sp	Bole & Twigs	-----	16	71	----	----	-----	-------	-----	---------
	Tomicus	*integer* Eichh.	Bole	-----	18	73	----	----	-----	-------	-----	---------
	Tomicus	*pini* Say.	Bole & Twigs	713	----	----	----	16	487	-------	-----	351

Damage to Pinus ponderosa and P. jeffreyi by Coleoptera

Family	Genus	Species	Parts Suffering	Literary References: 5th Rept. Ent. Com. U. S.	Ent. Bul. No. 48 U. S.	Ent. Bul. No. 53 U. S.	Ent. Bul. No. 32 U. S.	Ent. Bul No. 21 U. S.	Ent. Bul. No. 7 U. S.	Ag. Yr. Bk. for 1902 U. S.	Fld Prg For. Ser Apr. '07	The Forst'r for 1901	Ag. Yr Bk. for 1901 U. S.	Ent Bul No. 56 U. S.	Ag. Yr. Bk. for 1904 U. S.	St. Mus No. 8 N. Y.
Cerambycidæ	*Ergates*	*spiculatus* Lec.	Bole	704	21	77, 92	----	----	----	-----	---	---	-----	---	385	----
Scolytidæ	*Carphoborus*	n. sp.	Bole	-----	18	73	----	----	----	-----	---	---	-----	---	-----	----
	Dendroctonus	*approximatus* Dtz.	Bole	-----	44	----	----	----	----	-----	---	---	-----	---	-----	----
	Dendroctonus	*brevicomis* Lec.	Bole	722	18	74	----	20	----	-----	---	251	162	---	-----	----
	Dendroctonus	*monticolæ* Hopk.	Bole	-----	----	----	----	----	----	-----	21	---	162	---	-----	----
	Dendroctonus	*ponderosæ* Hopk	Bole	-----	44	100	all	----	----	275	---	251	162	all	-----	----
	Dendroctonus	*valens* Lec.	Bole	-----	19	74	12	----	----	-----	---	---	-----	---	-----	----
	Dendroctonus	n. sp.	Bole	-----	42, 44	101	----	----	----	-----	---	---	-----	---	-----	----
	Gnathotrichus	n. sp.	Bole	-----	15	70	[1]14	----	[2]30	-----	---	---	-----	---	-----	----
	Hylastes	*porosus* Er.	Rts. of S'd'ls.	-----	----	----	13	----	----	-----	---	---	-----	---	-----	----
	Hylurgops	*subcostulatus* Mann	Bole	-----	19	74	13	----	--	-----	---	---	-----	---	-----	----
	Pityogenes	*carniceps*	Bole	-----	----	----	14	----	----	-----	---	---	-----	---	-----	----
	Pityogenes	*carinulatus* Lec.	Bole	-----	17	72	----	----	----	-----	---	---	-----	---	-----	----
	Pityophthorus	*confinis* Lec.	Twigs	-----	16	71	----	----	----	-----	---	---	-----	---	-----	----
	Pityophthorus	*puncticollis* Lec.	Twigs	-----	16	72	----	----	----	-----	---	---	-----	---	-----	----
	Pityophthorus	n. sp.	Twigs	-----	16, 17	71, 72	----	----	----	-----	---	---	-----	---	-----	----
	Tomicus	*calligraphus* Germ	Bole	-----	----	----	11	----	----	-----	---	---	-----	---	-----	345
	Tomicus	*confusus* Lec.	Bole	-----	18	73	----	----	----	-----	---	---	-----	---	-----	----
	Tomicus	*integer* Eichh.	Bole	-----	18	73	----	----	----	-----	---	---	-----	---	-----	----
	Tomicus	*oregoni* Eichh.	Bole & Twigs	-----	17, 41, 44	73, 100	10	----	----	-----	---	---	-----	---	-----	----
Ptininidæ	?	?	Bole	-----	23	78	----	----	----	-----	---	---	-----	---	-----	----

[1]As *G. occidentalis* Hopk. Mss. [2]As *G. materiarius*.

Damage to Pinus rigida, P. echinata, P. tæda, P. palustris, and P. resinosa by Coleoptera

Family	Genus	Species	Parts Suffering	Literary References: 5th Rept Ent. Com. U. S	Ent Bul. No. 48 U S.	Ent. Bul No 53 U S	Ent Bul. No. 37 U. S.	Ent Bul No 32 U. S.	Ent Bul. No. 7 U. S.	Ag Yr Bk. for 1902 U. S	For. Rept. No 7 N. Y.	Ex Sta. No 56 W. Va.	Ex Sta. No 35 W. Va.	For Bul No. 22 U. S.	St Mus. No 8 N. Y.	Ag. Yr Bk. for 1905 U S
rambycidæ	*Acanthocinus*	*nodosus* Fab.	Bole	----	35	93	----	----	----	----	----	----	----	----	----	----
	Acanthocinus	*obsoletus* Oliv.	Bole	----	35	93	----	----	----	----	----	----	----	----	662	----
	Asemum	*mæstum* Hald	Bole	697	35	93	----	----	----	----	----	438	----	----	661	----
	**Callidium*	*antennatum* Newm	Bole	700	37	96	----	----	----	----	----	----	----	----	660	----
	Ceratographis	*pusillus* Kby.	Bole	----	35	93	----	----	----	----	----	----	----	----	----	----
	**Ergates*	*spiculatus* Lec.	Bole	704	35	93	----	----	----	----	----	----	----	----	----	----
	Monohammus	*confusor* Kby	Bole	686	35	93	----	----	----	----	494	----	----	----	360	----
	Monohammus	*scutellatus* Say.	Bole	696	35	93	----	----	----	----	----	----	300	----	364	----
	Orthosoma	*brunneum* De G.	Bole	702	----	----	----	----	----	----	----	----	----	----	487	----
	Prionus	*laticollis* Dru	Bole	----	37	95	----	----	----	----	----	----	----	----	486	----
	Rhagium	*lineatum* Oliv	Bole	704	37	96	----	----	----	----	492	439	----	----	366	----
uprestidæ	*Buprestis*	*apricans* Hbst.	Bole	----	39	97	----	----	----	----	----	----	----	----	----	----
	Buprestis	*aurulenta* Linn	Bole	----	39	98	----	----	----	----	----	----	----	----	----	----
	Chalcophora	*virginiensis* Dru	Bole	676	39	98	----	----	----	----	----	----	----	----	653	----
	Chrysobothris	*dentipes* Germ	Bole	680	38	97	----	----	----	----	512	----	----	----	----	----
urculionidæ	*Hylobius*	*pales* Hbst.	Bole & Twigs	724	34	92	----	----	----	----	500	441	----	----	664	----
	Pachylobius	*picivorus* Germ	Bole	727	34	92	----	----	----	----	----	----	----	----	----	----
	‡*Pissodes*	*strobi* Peck	Bole	734	34	91	----	----	----	----	497	----	----	----	397	252
hrysomelidæ	*Glyptoscelis*	*pubescens* Fab	Needles	----	----	----	----	----	----	----	509	----	----	----	----	----
olytidæ	*Crypturgus*	*pusillus*	Twigs	----	----	----	----	----	----	----	----	448	----	----	----	----
	***Dendroctonus*	*frontalis* Zimm	Bole	722	41, 44	100	----	----	73	270	480	----	----	----	----	----
	Dendroctonus	*obesus* Mann	Bole	----	----	----	22	----	----	----	----	----	----	----	----	----
	Dendroctonus	*terebrans* Oliv.	Bole	721	----	----	----	----	----	----	480	----	----	----	342	----
	Dendroctonus	*valens* Lec	Bole	----	----	----	----	12	----	----	----	----	----	----	----	----
	Gnathotrichus	*materiarius* Fitch.	Bole	718	----	----	----	----	30	----	----	442	----	----	371	----
	Hylurgops	*pinifex* Fitch	Bole	722	----	----	----	----	----	----	----	449	----	----	----	----
	Pityogenes	*plagiatus* Lec	?	----	----	----	----	----	----	----	----	447, 448	----	----	----	----
	Pityophthorus	?	Twigs	[1]715	----	----	----	----	----	----	----	442	----	57	----	----
	Tomicus	*avulsus* Eichh	Bole	----	41, 44	100	----	----	----	----	----	446	----	----	----	----
	Tomicus	*cacographus* Lec.	Twigs	713	----	----	----	----	----	----	485	445	----	56	356	----
	Tomicus	*calligraphus* Germ	Bole	711	----	----	----	----	----	----	482	----	----	----	354	----
	Tomicus	*cœlatus* Eichh	Bole	[2]706	----	----	----	12	----	----	488	----	----	----	345	----
	Tomicus	*pini* Say	Bole	713	----	----	----	----	----	----	487	445, 446	----	----	351	----
	Trypodendron	*bivittatum* Mannh	Bole	[3]720	16	----	----	----	[3]28	----	[3]495	----	----	----	369	----
	Xyleborus	*pubescens* Zimm	Bole	710	----	----	----	----	19	----	----	----	296	----	----	----

[1]As *P. annectens*? [2]As *Xyleborus* [3]As *Xyloterus bivittatus*

*Also Ag. Yr. Bk. for 1904, pp. 392 and 385. **Also Agr Yr Bk. for 1907, p 163. ‡See Entire Ent Cir No. 90, U S.

Damage to Larix occidentalis by Coleoptera

FAMILY	GENUS	SPECIES	PARTS SUFFERING	LITERARY REFERENCES			
				5th Rept. Ent. Com. U. S.	Ent. Bul. No. 48 U. S.	Ent. Bul. No. 53 U. S.	Ent. Bul. No. 21 U. S.
Buprestidæ	*Melanophila*	?	Bole	-----	-----	----	22
Scolytidæ	*Dendroctonus*	*similis* Lec.	Bole	722	19, 45	74	11, 22
	Dendroctonus	n. sp.	Bole	-----	19, 45	74	----
	Scolytus	*unispinosus* Lec.	Twigs	-----	20	76	16, 22

Damage to Picea spp. (eastern) by Coleoptera

Family	Genus	Species	Parts Suffering	Literary References													
				5th Rept. Ent. Com. U. S.	Ent. Bul. No. 48 U. S.	Ent. Bul. No. 53 U. S.	St. Mus. No. 8 N. Y.	Ent. Bul. No. 28 U. S.	Ent. Bul. No 7 U. S.	For Bul No 22 U. S.	Ag. Yr Bk. for 1902 U. S.	For. Rept. No. 7 N. Y.	Ex. Sta. No 56 W. Va	Ex. Sta No. 35 W. Va.	The Forester for 1901	Ent. Cir. No. 90 U. S.
Cerambycidæ	*Asemum*	*mæstum* Hald.	Bole	697	35	93	661	----	----	---	-----	-----	---	---	-----	----
	Leptura	*canadensis* Fab.	Bole	871	37	96	670	----	----	---	-----	-----	---	---	-----	----
	Monohammus	*confusor* Kby.	Bole	686	35	92	360	----	----	---	-----	494	---	---	-----	----
	Rhagium	*lineatum* Oliv.	Bole	704	37	97	366	----	----	---	-----	492	---	---	-----	----
	Tetropium	*cinnamopterum* Kby.	Bole	-----	37, 27	96, 83	----	27	----	---	-----	-----	259	---	-----	----
Buprestidæ	*Buprestis*	*aurulenta* Linn.	Bole	-----	39	98	----	----	----	---	-----	-----	---	---	-----	----
	Chalcophora	*virginiensis* Dru.	Bole	676	39	98	653	----	----	58	-----	-----	---	---	-----	----
Melandryidæ	*Serropalpus*	*barbatus* Schall.	Bole	-----	27	83	671	----	----	---	-----	-----	440	---	-----	----
Curculionidæ	**Pissodes*	*strobi* Peck.	Twigs	734	34	91	397	----	----	59	-----	497	---	---	-----	all
Scolytidæ	*Cryphalus*	n. sp.	Twigs	-----	24	79	----	----	----	---	-----	[4]516	---	---	-----	----
	Crypturgus	*atomus* Lec	Twigs	825	26	82	359	----	----	---	-----	-----	---	---	-----	----
	†*Dendroctonus*	*frontalis* Zimm.	Bole	722	44	----	----	----	----	55	270	480	245	---	-----	----
	†*Dendroctonus*	*piceaperda* Hopk	Bole	811	26	82	379	15	----	---	266	-----	230	---	250	----
	Dryocœtes	*autographus* Ratz.	Bole	-----	----	----	----	----	----	---	-----	[5]516	445	---	-----	----
	Dryocœtes	*granicollis* Lec.	Bole	-----	----	----	----	----	----	---	-----	[5]516	445	---	-----	----
	Dryocœtes	n. sp	Bole	-----	25	81	----	----	----	---	-----	-----	---	---	-----	----
	Gnathotrichus	*materiarius* Fitch.	Bole	718	15	70	371	----	30	57	-----	495	---	---	-----	----
	***Pterocyclon*	*mali* Fitch.	Bole	-----	----	----	----	----	[3]28	---	-----	[3]517	---	---	-----	----
	Pityophthorus	*carniceps* Lec	Twigs	-----	24	80	----	----	----	---	-----	-----	---	---	-----	----
	Pityophthorus	n. sp.	Twigs	715	24	80	----	----	----	---	-----	-----	442	---	-----	----
	Polygraphus	*rufipennis* Kby.	Bole	721	25	81	386	26	----	---	-----	513	349	---	-----	----
	Scolytus	n. sp	Twigs	-----	26	82	----	----	----	---	-----	-----	---	---	-----	----
	Tomicus	*balsameus* Lec.	Bole	-----	25	81	375	----	----	---	-----	519	---	---	-----	----
	Tomicus	*cacographus* Lec.	?	713	----	----	356	----	----	56	-----	485	---	---	-----	----
	Tomicus	*pini* Say.	Bole & Twigs	713	----	----	351	----	----	---	-----	487	---	---	-----	----
	Tomicus	n. sp	Bole	-----	25	81	----	----	----	---	-----	-----	---	---	-----	----
	Trypodendron	*bivittatum* Mann	Bole	[1]720, 823	----	----	369	----	[1]28	---	-----	[1]495	[2]256	295	-----	----
	Xyleborus	*cælatus* Zimm.	Bole	824, 812	----	----	----	----	----	---	-----	-----	---	---	-----	----
	Xylochinus	n. sp.	Bole	-----	26	81	----	----	----	---	-----	-----	---	---	-----	----
	Xyloterus	*politus* Say.	Bole	387	----	----	292	----	28	---	-----	516	---	---	-----	----

[1]As *Xyloterus bivittatus* [2]As *Xyloterus lineatus.* [3]As *Monarthrum* [4]As *C. striatulus* [5]As *D. species.*

*Also Ag. Yr. Bk. for 1905, p. 252. **Also Ent. Cir. No. 82, U. S., p. 2 (As *Monarthrum*). †Also Ag. Yr. Bk. for 1907, pp. 160 and 162.

Damage to Picea sitchensis and P. engelmanni by Coleoptera

Family	Genus	Species	Parts Suffering	Literary References									
				5th Rept. Ent. Com. U. S.	Ent. Bul. No. 48 U. S.	Ent. Bul. No 53 U. S.	Ent. Bul. No 37 U. S.	Ent. Bul. No. 21 U. S.	Ent. Bul. No. 7 U. S.	F'ld. Pr'g'm. For. S'ce. April, 1907	For. Rept. No. 7 N. Y.	Ag. Yr. Bk. for 1907 U. S.	St. Mus. Mem. No. 8 N. Y.
Curculionidæ	*Pissodes*	?	Twigs	----	34	91	----	----	----	----	----	----	----
Scolytidæ	*Carphoborus*	n. sp	Bole	----	18	73	----	----	----	----	----	----	----
	Dendroctonus	*engelmanni* Hopk.	Bole	----	----	----	----	----	----	22	----	161	----
	Dendroctonus	*obesus* Mann.	Bole	----	----	----	22	----	----	----	----	----	----
	Dolurgus	*pumilis* Mann.	Bole	----	18	73	----	----	----	----	----	----	----
	Dryocœtes	*affaber* Mann.	Bole	----	----	----	----	21	----	----	----	----	----
	Hylurgops	*rugipennis* Mann	Bole	----	19	74	----	21	----	----	----	----	----
	Pityophthorus	*nitidulus* Mann.	Twigs	----	17	72	----	----	----	----	----	----	----
	Pityophthorus	*puncticollis* Lec	Twigs	----	16	72	----	----	----	----	----	----	----
	Tomicus	*concinnus* Mann.	Bole	----	17	73	----	----	----	----	----	----	----
	Trypodendron	*bivittatum* Kby.	Bole	[1]720	16	71	----	[1]21	[1]28	----	[1]495	----	[1]369

[1]As *Xyloterus bivittatus* Mann.

Damage to Tsuga canadensis by Coleoptera

Family	Genus	Species	Parts Suffering	Literary References: 5th Rept. Ent. Com. U. S.	Ent. Bul. No. 48 U. S.	Ent. Bul. No. 53 U. S.	Ent. Bul. No. 37 U. S.	Ent. Bul. No. 21 U. S.	Ent Bul. No. 7 U. S.	For. Rept. No. 7 N. Y.	Ex. Sta. Bul. No. 56 W. Va.	Ag. Yr Bk for 1904 U. S.	St. Mus. Mem. No. 8 N. Y.
Cerambycidæ	*Leptura*	*canadensis* Fab.	Bole	871	37	96	----	----	----	-----	-------	-----	670
	Xylotrechus	*undulatus* Say	Bole	830	37	96	----	----	----	-----	-------	-----	671
Buprestidæ	*Melanophila*	*fulvoguttata* Harr.	Bole	684	38	97	22	17	----	-----	255	-----	390
Scolytidæ	*Trypodendron*	*bivittatum* Kby	Bole	823	16	71	----	[1]21	[1]28	[1]495	[2]256	383	[1]369
	Xyleborus	*obesus* Lec.	Bole	----	----	----	----	----	23	-----	-------	-----	---------
	Xyleborus	*saxeseni* Ratz.	Bole	706	16	71	----	----	[3]24	-----	-------	-----	---------

[1]As *Xyloterus bivittatus*. [2]As *Xyloterus lineatus*. [3]As *X. xylographus*.

Damage to Tsuga heterophylla by Coleoptera

Family	Genus	Species	Parts Suffering	Literary References								
				5th Rept. Ent. Com. U. S.	Ent. Bul. No. 48 U. S.	Ent. Bul. No. 53 U. S.	Ent. Bul. No. 7 U. S.	Ent. Bul. No. 21 U. S.	Ent. Bul. No. 37 U. S.	For. Rept. No. 7 N. Y.	The Forester for 1901	St. Mus. Mem. No. 8 N. Y.
Buprestidæ	*Asemum*	*nitidum* Lec.	Bole		21	76						
	Melanophila	*drummondi* Kby.	Bole	685	22, 38	77, 97		17	22		251	
Scolytidæ	*Gnathotrichus*	*sulcatus* Lec.	Bole		15	70						
	Hylesinus	n. sp.	Bole		20	75					[2]251	
	Platypus	n. sp.	Bole		15	70						
	Trypodendron	*bivittatum* Kby.	Bole		16	71	[1]28			[1]495		[1]369

[1]As *Xyloterus bivittatus*. [2]As *Hylesinus tsuga* Hopk. Mss.

Damage to Pseudotsuga by Coleoptera

Family	Genus	Species	Parts Suffering	Literary References: 5th Rept. Ent. Com. U. S.	Ent. Bul. No. 48 U. S.	Ent. Bul. No. 53 U. S.	Ent. Bul. No. 37 U. S.	Ent. Bul. No. 21 U. S.	The Forester for 1901	St. Mus. No. 8 N. Y.
Cerambycidæ	*Xylotrechus*	*undulatus* Say	Bole	830	37	96	----	----	------	671
Buprestidæ	*Asemum*	*nitidum* Lec.	Bole	-----	21	76	22	----	251	---------
	Melanophila	*drummondi* Kby.	Bole	685	22, 38	77, 97	----	17	251	---------
Scolytidæ	*Carphoborus*	n. sp.	Bole	-----	18	73	----	----	------	---------
	Dendroctonus	*pseudotsugæ* Hopk	Bole	-----	----	----	----	----	251	---------
	Dendroctonus	*similis* Lec.	Bole	722	19	74	----	10	------	---------
	Gnathotrichus	*sulcatus* Lec.	Bole	-----	15	70	----	----	------	---------
	Hylesinus	*nebulosus* Lec.	Bole	-----	20	75	----	----	------	---------
	Hylesinus	n. sp.	Bole	-----	19	75	----	----	------	---------
	Pityophthorus	*nitidulus* Mann.	Twigs	-----	17	72	----	----	------	---------
	Platypus	n. sp.	Bole	-----	15	70	----	----	------	---------
	Scolytus	*unispinosus* Lec.	Bole	850	20	76	----	16, 21	------	---------
	Xyleborus	*saxeseni* Ratz.	Bole	-----	16	71	----	----	------	---------

Damage to Abies grandis and A. concolor by Coleoptera

Family	Genus	Species	Parts Suffering	Literary References: 5th Rept. Ent. Com. U. S.	Ent. Bul. No. 48 U. S.	Ent. Bul. No. 53 U. S.	Ent. Bul. No. 21 U. S.	The Forester for 1901	St. Mus. Mem. No. 8 N. Y.
Cerambycidæ	*Xylotrechus*	*undulatus* Say	Bole	830	37	96	----	------	671
Scolytidæ	*Cryphalus*	n. sp.	Bole	-----	16	71	----	------	---------
	Gnathotrichus	*sulcatus* Lec.	Bole	-----	15	70	----	------	---------
	Hylesinus	*granulatus* Lec.	Bole	-----	19	75	----	------	---------
	Hylesinus	n. sp.	Bole	-----	19, 20	75	----	------	---------
	Pityogenes	n. sp.	Bole	-----	17	72	----	------	---------
	Pityophthorus	n. sp.	Twigs	-----	17	72	----	------	---------
	Scolytus	*præceps* Lec.	Bole	-----	21	76	26	------	---------
	Scolytus	*subscaber* Lec.	Bole	-----	21	76	----	251	---------
	Scolytus	n. sp.	Bole	-----	20	76	----	------	---------
	Tomicus	n. sp.	Bole	-----	17	72	----	------	---------

Damage to Abies fraseri and A. balsamea by Coleoptera

Family	Genus	Species	Parts Suffering	Literary References: Ent. Bul. No. 48 U. S.	Ent. Bul. No. 53 U. S.	For. Rept. No. 7 N. Y.	Ex. Sta. Bul. No. 56 W. Va.	Ag. Yr. Bk. for 1905 U. S.	St. Mus. Mem. No. 8 N. Y.
Melandryidæ	*Serropalpus*	*barbatus* Schall.	Bole	27[1]	83	-----	440	------	671
Cerambycidæ	*Pachyta*	*monticola* Rand.	Bole	----	----	-----	--------	------	---------
Buprestidæ	*Buprestis*	*aurulenta* Linn.	Bole	39	98	-----	--------	------	---------
Curculionidæ	*Pissodes*	*dubius* Rand.	Bole	34	92	-----	--------	254	401
Scolytidæ	*Cryphalus*	n. sp.	Twigs	24	79	-----	--------	------	---------
	Tomicus	*balsameus* Lec.	Bole	25	81	519	--------	------	375
	Xylochinus	n. sp.	Bole	26	81	-----	--------	------	---------

[1] As *S. varbatus* (a typographical error).

Damage to Taxodium distichum by Coleoptera

Family	Genus	Species	Parts Suffering	Literary References: 5th Rept. Ent. Com. U. S.	Ent. Bul. No. 48 U. S.	Ent. Bul. No. 53 U. S.	Ent. Bul. No. 7 U. S.	Ex. Sta. Bul. No. 35 W. Va.	Ent. Cir. No. 82 U. S.	Ag. Yr. Bk. for 1904 U. S.	St. Mus. Mem. No. 8 N. Y.
Cerambycidæ	*Curius*	*dentatus* Newm.	Twigs	----	36	95	----	----	----	----	----
	Neoclytus	*erythrocephalus* Fab.	Bole	----	37	96	----	----	----	----	71
	Oeme	*rigida* Say	Bole	----	46, 37	95, 102	----	----	----	----	----
	Physocnemum	*andreæ* Hald.	Bole	----	46, 36	94	----	----	----	----	----
Buprestidæ	*Acmæo*	*pulchella* Hbst.	Bole	----	46, 39	----	----	----	----	----	----
Curculionidæ	*Eudocimus*	*mannerheimii* Boh.	Bole & Twigs	----	46, 34	92	----	----	----	----	----
Brenthidæ	*Eupsalis*	*minuta* Dru.	Bole	----	39	98	----	----	----	----	261
Scolytidæ	*Phlœosinus*	n. sp.	Bole	----	46, 42	101	----	----	----	----	----
	Platypus	*compositus* Say	Bole	18	45, 39	----	14	----	2	----	----
	Pterocyclon	*fasciatum* Say	Bole	----	45	----	[1]26	----	----	----	----
	Pterocyclon	*mali* Fitch	Bole	----	45	----	[1]27	295	----	384	[1]289
	Xyleborus	n. sp.	Bole	----	45	----	----	----	----	----	----

[1] As *Monarthrum*.

Damage to Sequoia by Coleoptera

Family	Genus	Species	Parts Suffering	Literary References			
				Ent. Bul. No. 48 U. S.	Ent. Bul. No. 53 U. S.	Ent. Bul. No. 37 U. S.	For. Bul. No. 38 U. S.
Cerambycidæ	*Phymatodes*	*decussatus* Lec.		----	----	----	39
Scolytidæ	*Phlœosinus*	*cupressi* Hopk.	Twigs	----	----	----	35
	Phlœosinus	*sequoiæ* Hopk.	Bole	18, 45	74	23	33

Damage to Thuja gigantea by Coleoptera

Family	Genus	Species	Parts Suffering	Literary References				
				5th Rept. Ent. Com. U. S.	Ent. Bul. No. 48 U. S.	Ent. Bul. No. 53 U. S.	Ent. Bul. No. 37 U. S.	Ent. Bul. No. 21 U. S.
Cerambycidæ	*Callidium*	*janthinum* Lec.	Bole	809	----	----	23	21
	Hylotrupes	*amethystinus* Lec.	Bole	------	21	77	----	----
Scolytidæ	*Gnathotrichus*	*sulcatus* Lec.	Bole	------	15	70	----	----
	Phlœosinus	*punctatus* Lec.	Bole	------	18	73	----	----
	Phlœosinus	*sequoiæ* Hopk.	Bole	------	18, 45	74	----	----
Ptinidæ	*Dryophilus*	?	Bole	------	23	78	----	----
	?	?	Bole	------	23	78	----	----

Damage to Chamæcyparis lawsoniana by Coleoptera

Family	Genus	Species	Parts Suffering	Literary References		
				Ent. Bul. No. 48 U. S.	Ent. Bul. No 53 U. S.	Far. Bul. No. 38 U. S.
Scolytidæ	*Phlœosinus*	*cupressi* Hopk.	Twigs	41, 45	100	35
	Phlœosinus	*punctatus* Lec.	Bole	18	73	------

Damage to Chamæcyparis by Coleoptera

Family	Genus	Species	Parts Suffering	Literary References					
				5th Rept Ent. Com. U. S.	Ent. Bul. No. 48 U. S.	Ent. Bul. No. 53 U. S	Ent. Bul No. 37 U S	For. Rept. No. 7 N. Y.	St. Mus. Mem. No. 8 N. Y.
Cerambycidæ	*Hylotrupes*	*ligneus* Fab.	Bole	-----	27, 38	83, 96	23	------	675
Scolytidæ	*Phlœosinus*	*dentatus* Say	Bole	905	----	----	----	522	391

Damage to Juniperus virginiana by Coleoptera

Family	Genus	Species	Parts Suffering	Literary References					
				Ent. Bul. No. 48 U. S.	Ent. Bul. No. 53 U. S.	Ent. Bul. No. 37 U. S.	Ex. Sta. Bul. No. 56 W. Va.	Ag.Yr.Bk. for 1904 U. S.	St. Mus. Mem. No. 8 N. Y.
Cerambycidæ	*Callidium*	*antennatum* Newm	Bole	37	96	----	438	392	660
	Hylotrupes	*ligneus* Fab.	Bole	38, 27	83, 96	23	--------	-----	675
Scolytidæ	*Phlœosinus*	*dentatus* Lec.	Bole	25	81	----	--------	-----	391

Damage to Juglans by Coleoptera

Family	Genus	Species	Parts Suffering	Literary References			
				5th Rept. Ent. Com. U. S.	Ent. Bul. No. 48 U. S.	Ent. Bul. No. 53 U. S.	St. Mus Mem. No. 8 N. Y.
Cerambycidæ	*Gauroles*	*cyanipennis* Say	Bole	-----	36	94	---------
	Urographis	*fasciatus* Horn	Bole	-----	38	96	434
Curculionidæ	*Attelabus*	*analis* Web	Leaves	335	----	----	---------
	Conotrachelus	*juglandis* Lec	Fruit	335	33	90	581
	Cryptorhynchus	*parochus* Hbst	Bole	-----	34	92	---------
Scarabæidæ	*Allorhina*	*nitida* Linn	Bole	329	----	----	---------

Damage to Hicoria spp. by Coleoptera

Family	Genus	Species	Parts Suffering	Literary References: 5th Rept Ent. Com. U S	Ent. Bul. No. 48 U. S.	Ent Bul. No. 53 U. S.	Ent. Bul No. 37 U S.	Ent Bul No. 7 U S.	Ent. Cir. No. 55 U. S.	Ent Bul No. 21 U. S.	Ag Yr. Bk for 1903 U. S.	Geo Rpt for 1899 N. J.	Ag. Yr. Bk. for 1904 U S.	Ag Yr Bk. for 1907 U. S.	St Mus. No. 8 N. Y.
Cerambycidæ	*Chion*	*cinctus* Dru.	Bole	287	36	94	----	----	----	----	----	----	----	----	267
	Cyllene	*picta* Dru	Bole	287, 356	36	94	----	----	----	----	----	----	----	----	264
	Eburia	*quadrigeminata* Sy	Bole	----	38	96	----	----	----	----	----	----	----	----	462
	Elaphidion	*villosum* Fab.	Twigs	83	34	91	----	----	----	----	----	----	----	----	59
	Goes	*oculatus* Lec	Bole	286	----	----	----	----	----	----	----	----	----	----	----
	Goes	*pulchra* Hald.	Bole	286	36	94	----	----	----	----	----	----	----	----	431
	Goes	*tigrina* De G	Bole	285	36	94	----	----	----	----	----	----	----	----	----
	Mallodon	*dasystomus* Say	Bole	----	37	95	----	----	----	----	----	----	----	----	----
	Neoclytus	*erythrocephalus* Fb	Bole	----	37	96	----	----	----	----	----	----	----	----	71
	Oncideres	*cingulata* Say	Twigs	288	34	92	----	----	----	----	----	----	----	----	271
	Saperda	*discoidea* Fab.	Bole	287	36	94	----	----	----	----	----	----	----	----	269
	Urographis	*fasciatus* Horn	Bole	----	38	96	----	----	----	----	----	----	----	----	431
	Xylotrechus	*colonus* Fab.	Bole	----	38	96	----	----	----	----	----	----	----	----	259
Buprestidæ	*Chrysobothris*	*femorata* Fab.	Bole	291, 64	38	97	----	----	----	----	----	----	----	----	86
	Dicerca	*lurida* Fab	Bole & Twigs	290	----	----	----	----	----	----	----	----	----	----	442
	Dicerca	*obscura* Fab.	Bole & Twigs	----	38	97	----	----	----	----	----	----	----	----	----
Curculionidæ	*Balaninus*	*nasicus* Say	Fruit	327	33	90	----	----	----	----	----	----	----	----	583
	Balaninus	*rectus* Say	Fruit	327	----	----	----	----	----	----	----	----	302	----	585
	Conotrachelus	*elegans* Say	Lvs. & Fruit?	316	----	----	----	----	----	----	----	----	----	----	----
	Conotrachelus	*nenuphar* Herbst.	Lvs. & Fruit?	316	----	----	----	----	----	----	----	----	----	----	----
Scolytidæ	*Chramesus*	*icoriæ* Lec.	Twigs	296	----	----	----	----	----	----	----	----	----	----	----
	Scolytus	*quadrispinosus* Sy.	Bole & Twigs	294	41	101	25	----	----	15	314	218	----	163	275
	Xyleborus	*celsus* Eichh.	Bole	----	39	98	----	23	----	----	----	----	384	----	446
	Xyleborus	*saxeseni* Ratz.	Bole	706	16	71	----	[1]24	----	----	----	----	----	----	----
Chrysomeilidæ	*Systena*	*marginalis* Ill.	Leaves	316	----	----	----	----	----	----	----	----	----	----	515
Ptinidæ	*Lyctus*	spp.	Bole & Twigs	----	39	98	26	----	----	----	----	----	----	----	----
	Sinoxylon	*basilare* Say.	Bole & Twigs	[2]296	39	98	----	----	all	----	----	----	387	----	442

[1]As *X. xylographus*. [2]As *Apate*.

Damage to Populus spp. by Coleoptera

Family	Genus	Species	Parts Suffering	Literary References: 5th Rept. Ent. Com. U. S.	Ent. Bul. No. 48 U. S.	Ent. Bul. No. 53 U. S.	Ent. Bul. No. 7 U. S.	Ent. Bul. No. 38 U. S.	For. Bul. No. 46 U. S.	Ag. Yr. Bk. for 1903 U. S.	Ex. Sta. Bul. No. 234 Cornell	St. Mus. Mem. No. 8 N. Y.
Cerambycidæ	*Mecas*	*inornata* Say	Bole	427	----	----	----	----	----	-----	--------	---------
	Prionus	*laticollis* Dru.	Bole	437	----	----	----	----	----	-----	--------	486
	Saperda	*calcarata* Say	Bole	435	35	93	----	----	----	-----	--------	98
	Saperda	*concolor* Lec.	Bole	436	35	93	----	----	66	-----	--------	474
Buprestidæ	*Agrilus*	*anxius* Gory	Bole	-----	21, 38	77, 97	----	----	67	[4]322	all	284
Scarabæidæ	*Cotalpa*	*lanigera* Linn.	Leaves	-----	32	89	----	----	----	-----	--------	---------
Chrysomelidæ	*Phytodecta*	*pallida* Linn.	Leaves	[1]470	----	----	----	----	77	-----	--------	---------
	Melasoma	*lapponica* Linn.	Leaves	-----	----	----	----	----	77	-----	--------	---------
	Melasoma	*scripta* Fab.	Leaves	[2]428	32	90	----	[2]37	74	-----	--------	317
Scolytidæ	*Xyleborus*	*saxeseni* Ratz.	Bole	706	16	71	[3]24	----	----	-----	--------	---------

[1]As *Chrysomela*. [2]As *Lina*. [3]As *X. xylographus*. [4]As *Agrilus* sp.

Damage to Betula spp. by Coleoptera

Family	Genus	Species	Parts Suffering	Literary References						
				5th Rept Ent. Com. U. S.	Ent. Bul. No. 48 U. S	Ent. Bul No. 53 U. S.	For Bul. No. 46 U. S.	Ag. Yr Bk. for 1903 U. S.	Ex Sta. Bul. No. 234 Cornell	St. Mus. Mem. No. 8 N. Y.
Cerambycidæ	*Bellamira*	*scalaris* Say	Bole	486	----	----	----	----	----	----
Buprestidæ	*Agrilus*	*anxius* Gory	Bole	----	21, 38	77, 97	67	[2]322	all	284
	Chrysobothris	*6-signata* Say	Bole	485	----	----	----	----	----	----
Scolytidæ	*Dryocœtes*	*eichhoffi* Hopk.	Bole	----	[1]25	[1]81	----	320	----	----
	Pityophthorus	n. sp.	Twigs	----	24	80	----	----	----	----
	Trypodendron	n. sp	Bole	----	16	71	----	----	----	----

[1]As *Dryocœtes* n. sp. [2]As *Agrilus* sp.

Damage to Fagus spp. by Coleoptera

Family	Genus	Species	Parts Suffering	Literary References: 5th Rept. Ent. Com. U. S.	Ent. Bul. No. 48 U. S.	Ent Bul. No. 53 U. S.	Ent. Bul. No 7 U. S.	Ag. Yr Bk for 1903 U. S.	For. Rept. No 7 N. Y.	Ex. Sta. Bul. No. 35 W. Va.	St. Mus. Mem. No. 8 N. Y.
Cerambycidæ	*Goes*	*pulverulentus* Hld.	Twigs	515	----	----	----	-----	-----	---------	455
Buprestidæ	*Brachys*	*æruginosa* Gory	Leaves	519	----	----	----	-----	-----	---------	---------
Scolytidæ	*Corthylus*	*columbianus* Hpk.	Bole	-----	----	----	17	327	-----	---------	---------
	Pterocyclon	*mali* Fitch	Bole	-----	45	----	[1]27	-----	[1]517	295	---------
	Xyleborus	*saxeseni* Ratz.	Bole	706	16	71	[2]24	-----	-----	---------	---------
	Xyloterus	*politus* Say	Bole	-----	----	----	28	-----	516	---------	---------
Brenthidæ	*Eupsalis*	*minuta* Dru.	Bole	-----	39	98	----	323	-----	---------	261

[1]As *Monarthrum*. [2]As *X. xylographus*.

Damage to Castanea spp. by Coleoptera

Family	Genus	Species	Parts Suffering	Literary References: 5th Rept. Ent. Com. U. S.	Ent. Bul. No. 48 U. S.	Ent. Bul. No. 53 U. S.	Ent. Bul. No 37 U. S.	Ent. Bul. No. 7 U. S.	Ag. Yr. Bk. for 1903 U. S.	Geo Rpt for 1899 N. J.	Ex. Sta. No. 35 W. Va.	The Forst'r for 1901	Ent Cir. No. 82 U. S.	Ag. Yr. Bk. for 1904 U. S.	Ag. Yr. Bk. for 1904 U. S.	St. Mus. No. 8 N. Y.
erambycidæ	*Arhopalus*	*fulminans* Fab.	Bole	343	37	95	----	----	-----	----	---	---	---	-----	-----	444
	Callidium	*æreum* Newm.	Bole	-----	36	94	----	----	-----	----	---	---	---	-----	-----	----
	Chion	*cinctus* Dru.	Bole	287	36	94	----	----	-----	----	---	---	---	-----	-----	267
	Prionus	*laticollis* Dru.	Bole	-----	----	----	23	----	-----	----	---	---	---	-----	-----	486
	Urographis	*fasciatus* De G.	Bole	354	38	96	----	71	-----	----	---	---	---	-----	-----	434
	Xylotrechus	*colonus* Fab.	Bole	-----	38	96	----	----	-----	----	---	---	---	-----	-----	139
uprestidæ	**Agrilus*	*bilineatus* Web.	Bole	222	38	97	24	69	321	----	---	---	---	-----	-----	280
	Chrysobothris	*femorata* Fab.	Bole	-----	38	----	----	----	-----	----	---	---	---	-----	-----	86
urculionidæ	*Balaninus*	*proboscideus* Fab.	Fruit	-----	----	----	----	----	-----	----	---	---	---	301	-----	----
	Balaninus	*rectus* Say	Fruit	-----	----	----	----	----	-----	----	---	---	---	302	-----	----
	Balaninus	?	Fruit	350	33	97	----	----	-----	228	---	---	---	-----	-----	----
	Cryptorhynchus	?	Bole	-----	----	----	----	[2]71	-----	----	---	---	---	-----	-----	----
ymexylidæ	*Hylecœtus*	*lugubris* Say	Bole	[1]81	----	----	----	----	-----	----	292	---	---	-----	386	----
	Lymexylon	*sericeum* Harr.	Bole	-----	40	98	24	----	325	----	292	---	---	-----	-----	449
renthidæ	*Eupsalis*	*minuta* Dru.	Bole	-----	39	98	24	----	323	----	294	---	---	-----	386	261
colytidæ	*Platypus*	*compositus* Say	Bole	18	39	----	----	14	-----	----	---	---	2	-----	-----	----
	Xyleborus	*pubescens* Zimm.	Bole	710	----	----	----	19	-----	----	206	251	---	-----	-----	----

[1]As *americanus* Harr. [2]As *C. bisignatus* Say. *See entire Ent. Cir. No. 24, U. S.

Damage to Quercus spp. by Coleoptera

Family	Genus	Species	Parts Suffering	Literary References: 5th Rept. Ent Com. U. S.	Ent. Bul. No 48 U. S.	Ent Bul. No 53 U. S.	Ent Bul. No. 37 U. S.	Ent. Bul. No. 7 U. S.	Ag. Yr Bk. for 1903 U. S.	Geo Rpt for 1899 N. J.	For Rpt No. 7 N. Y.	Ex. Sta. No. 56 W. Va.	Ex. Sta. No. 35 W. Va.	The Forester for 1901	Ent. Cir No. 82 U. S.	St. Mus. No. 8 N. Y.
Cerambycidæ	*Arhopalus*	*fulminans* Fab.	Bole	74	37	95										444
	Chion	*cinctus* Dru	Bole		36	94										267
	Elaphidion	*villosum* Fab.	Twigs	83	34	91				216						59
	Goes	*tesselata* Hald.	Bole							220						
	Goes	*tigrina* De G	Bole		36											268
	Graphisurus	*fasciatus* De G.	Bole	71												
	Mallodon	*dasystomus* Say	Bole	79	37	95										
	Mallodon	*melanopus* Linn	Bole	50	37	95										
	Oncideres	*cingulata* Say	Twigs	288	34	92										239
	**Phymatodes*	*variabilis* Linn.	Bole	74						223						433
	Prionus	*laticollis* Dru	Bole	52	37	95	23			219						486
	Urographis	*fasciatus* Horn	Bole		38	69										434
	Xylotrechus	*colonus* Fab	Bole	77	38	96										271
Buprestidæ	‡*Agrilus*	*bilineatus* Web.	Bole		38	97	24		321			255				280
	Chrysobothris	*femorata* Fab.	Bole	64	38	97										86
Curculionidæ	*Balaninus*	*nasicus* Say	Fruit	216	33	90					531					583
	Ithycerus	*noveboracensis* Fst	Twigs	94												517
	Magdalis	*olyra* Herbst	Bole	80												261
Brenthidæ	**Eupsalis*	*minuta* Dru.	Bole	69	39	98	24		323					250		274
Lymexilidæ	*Hylecœtus*	*americanus* Harr	Bole	81									297			
	Lymexylon	*sericeum* Harr.	Bole	81	40	98	24		325							449
Scarabæidæ	*Cotalpa*	*lanigera* Linn	Leaves		32	89										
Chrysomelidæ	*Serica*	*trociformis* Burm	Leaves								528					
Scolytidæ	*Corthylus*	*columbianus* Hopk	Bole				24	17	327							
	**Pterocyclon*	*mali* Fitch	Bole		45			[2]28			[2]517		295		[2]2	
	Pityophthorus	*minutissimus* Zim.	Bole		24	80										295
	Pityophthorus	*pruinosus* Eichh.	Bole						318							
	Pityophthorus	*pubipennis* Lec	Bole	93	16	71										
	Pityophthorus	*querciperda* Schw.	Bole	93												
	Platypus	*compositus* Say	Bole	18	39	98		14							2	
	Xyleborus	*celsus* Eich	Bole	92	39	98		24								446
	Xyleborus	*fuscatus* Eichh.	Bole	93				21								
	Xyleborus	*obesus* Lec.	Bole	93[1]				23								
	Xyleborus	*saxeseni* Ratz.	Bole	706	16	71		[3]24								

[1]As *X. retusicollis*. [2]As *Monarthrum*. [3]As *X. xylographus*. *Also Ag. Yr. Bk. for 1904, pp. 398, 386, and 384. ‡See Entire Ent. Cir No. 24, U. S.

Damage to Ulmus spp. by Coleoptera

Family	Genus	Species	Parts Suffering	Literary References										
				5th Rept. Ent. Com. U. S.	Ent. Bul. No. 48 U. S.	Ent. Bul No. 53 U. S.	Ent. Bul. No. 37 U. S.	Ag. Yr. Bk. for 1903 U. S.	Far. Bul. No. 99 U. S.	Geol. Rept. for 1899 N. J.	Ag. Yr. Bk. for 1895 U. S.	St. Mus. Bul. No. 109 N. Y.	St. Mus. Bul. No. 53 N. Y.	St. Mus. Mem. No. 8 N. Y.
ambycidæ	*Saperda*	*tridentata* Oliv.	Bole	-----	35	93	32	-----	----	------	-----	--------	--------	67
nthidæ	*Eupsalis*	*minuta* Dru.	Bole	-----	39	98	----	-----	----	------	-----	--------	--------	261
ysomelidæ	*Galerucella*	*luteola* Mull.	Leaves	[1]234	32	90	----	-----	7	207	363	9	738	146
	Monocesta	*coryli* Say	Leaves	-----	32	90	----	-----	----	------	-----	--------	--------	--------
lytidæ	*Hylastinus*	*rufipes* Eichh.	Bole	-----	----	----	----	320	----	------	-----	--------	--------	--------
culionidæ	*Magdalis*	*barbata* Say	Bole	-----	----	----	----	-----	----	------	-----	--------	--------	73
	Magdalis	*armicollis* Say	Bole	-----	----	----	----	-----	----	------	-----	--------	--------	75

[1]As *Galeruca xanthomelæna*.

Damage to Liriodendron by Coleoptera

Family	Genus	Species	Parts Suffering	Literary References				
				Ent. Bul. No. 48 U. S.	Ent. Bul No. 53 U. S.	Ent. Bul. No. 7 U. S.	Ag. Yr. Bk for 1903 U. S.	St. Mus. Mem. No. 8 N. Y.
Cerambycidæ	*Leptostylus*	*aculiferus* Say	Bole	36	----	----	-----	461
Scolytidæ	*Corthylus*	*columbianus* Hopk	Bole	----	----	17	327	---------
	Xyleborus	*dispar* Fab.	Bole & Twigs	----	----	22	-----	---------
	Xyleborus	*tachygraphus* Zim	Twigs	----	----	23, 79	-----	---------

Damage to Liquidambar spp. by Coleoptera

Family	Genus	Species	Parts Suffering	Literary References		
				Ent. Bul. No 48 U. S.	Ent. Bul. No. 53 U. S.	St. Mus. Mem. No. 8 N. Y.
Cerambycidæ	*Neoclytus*	*erythrocephalus* Fab.	Bole	37	96	71
	Urographis	*fasciatus* Horn.	Bole	38	96	434

Damage to Pyrus spp. by Coleoptera

Family	Genus	Species	Parts Suffering	Literary References: 5th Rept. Ent. Com. U. S.	Ent. Bul No. 48 U. S.	Ent. Bul No. 53 U. S.	Ent. Bul No. 7 U. S.	Ex. Sta. Bul. No. 56 W Va.	Ent. Cir. No. 29 U. S.	Ag. Yr. Bk. for 1904 U. S.	St. Mus. Mem. No. 8 N. Y.
Cerambycidæ	*Saperda*	?	Bole	-----	27	83	----	--------	----	-----	---------
Scolytidæ	*Pterocyclon*	*mali* Fitch	Bole	-----	45	----	[1]27	--------	----	[1]384	[1]289
	Scolytus	*rugulosus* Ratz.	Bole	-----	----	----	----	295	all	-----	453
	Xyleborus	*saxeseni* Ratz	Bole	706	16	71	[2]24	--------	----	-----	---------

[1]As *Monarthrum*. [2]As *X. xylographus*.

Damage to Robinia by Coleoptera

Family	Genus	Species	Parts Suffering	Literary References: 5th Rept. Ent. Com. U. S.	Ent. Bul. No. 48 U. S.	Ent. Bul. No. 53 U. S.	Geol. Rept. for 1899 N. J.	Ent. Cir. No. 83 U. S.	Ent. Bul No. 58 U. S.	Ag. Yr. Bk. for 1907 U. S.	Ins. Bul. No. 7 Ohio	St. Mus. Mem No. 8 N. Y.
Cerambycidæ	*Cyllene*	*robiniæ* Forst.	Bole	355	35	93	214	all	1, 31	164	8	93
Buprestidæ	*Agrilus*	*otiosus* Say	Leaves	367	----	----	------	----	----	-----	-----	---------
Curculionidæ	*Apion*	*nigrum* Hbst.	Fruit	[1]367	----	----	------	----	----	-----	23	---------
Chrysomelidæ	*Odontota*	*dorsalis* Thunb.	Leaves	-----	----	----	------	----	----	-----	15	325
	Odontota	*scutellaris* Oliv.	Leaves	367	----	----	------	----	----	-----	----	---------
	Crepidodera	*rufipes* Linn.	Leaves	-----	----	----	------	----	----	-----	21	---------

[1]As *A. rostrum*.

Damage to Acer spp. by Coleoptera

Family	Genus	Species	Parts Suffering	Literary References: 5th Rept. Ent. Com. U. S.	Ent. Bul No. 48 U. S.	Ent. Bul. No. 53 U. S.	Ent. Bul. No. 7 U. S.	For. Rept. No. 7 N. Y.	For. Rept. No. 4 N. Y.	Ex Sta Bul. No. 35 W. Va.	St. Mus. Mem No. 8 N. Y.
Cerambycidæ	*Elaphidion*	*villosum* Fab.	Twigs	83	34	91	----	-----	392	--------	59
	Neoclytus	*erythrocephala* Fab	Bole	-----	37	96	----	-----	-----	--------	--------
	Plagionotus	*speciosus* Say.	Bole	374	35	93	----	-----	386	--------	51
	Urographis	*fasciatus* Horn.	Bole	-----	38	96	----	-----	-----	--------	434
	Xylotrechus	*colonus* Fab	Bole	77	38	96	----	-----	-----	--------	239
Buprestidæ	*Chrysobothris*	*femorata* Fab.	Bole	385	38	97	----	-----	-----	--------	86
	Dicerca	*obscura* Fab	Bole & Twigs	-----	38	----	----	-----	-----	--------	--------
Ptinidæ	*Ptilinus*	*ruficornis* Say.	Bole	388	38	97	----	-----	-----	--------	298
Scolytidæ	*Corthylus*	*punctatissimus* Zm	Bole	389	----	----	16	-----	-----	--------	65
	Trypodendron	*fasciatum* Say.	Bole	-----	----	----	[2]28	-----	-----	--------	--------
	Trypodendron	*mali* Fitch	Bole	-----	----	----	[2]28	-----	-----	--------	--------
	Xyloterus	*politus* Say.	Bole	-----	----	----	28	516	-----	--------	292
	Xyleborus	*obesus* Lec.	Bole	-----	----	----	23	-----	-----	295	--------
	Xyleborus	*pubescens* Zimm.	Bole	710	----	----	19	-----	-----	--------	--------
	Xyleborus	*saxeseni* Ratz.	Bole	-----	16	71	24	-----	-----	--------	--------
	Xyleborus	*tachygraphus* Zim.	Bole	-----	----	----	23	-----	-----	--------	--------
	Xyleborus	*cælatus* Echh.	Bole	706	----	----	[3]26	-----	-----	--------	--------

[1]As *Glycobius*. [2]As *Monarthrum*. [3]As *X. xylographus*.

Damage to Tilia spp. by Coleoptera

Family	Genus	Species	Parts Suffering	Literary References					
				5th Rept. Ent. Com. U. S.	Ent. Bul. No. 48 U. S.	Ent. Bul. No. 53 U. S.	Ent. Bul No. 7 U. S.	Ent. Bul. No. 38 U. S.	St. Mus. Mem. No. 8 N. Y.
Cerambycidæ	*Saperda*	*vestita* Say	Bole	474	36	93	----	----	91
Chrysomelidæ	*Chrysomela*	*scalaris* Lec.	Leaves	479	----	----	----	----	---------
	Odontota	*rubra* Web.	Leaves	-----	----	----	----	83	---------
Scolytidæ	*Xyleborus*	*saxeseni* Ratz.	Bole	-----	16	71	[1]24	----	---------

[1]As *X. xylographus*.

Damage to Fraxinus spp. by Coleoptera

Family	Genus	Species	Parts Suffering	Literary References: 5th Rept. Ent. Com. U. S.	Ent. Bul. No. 48 U. S.	Ent. Bul. No. 53 U. S.	Ent. Bul. No. 38 U. S.	Ent. Cir. No. 55 U. S.	Ag. Yr. Bk. for 1903 U. S.	Ag. Yr. Bk. for 1904 U. S.	St. Mus. Mem. No. 8 N. Y.
Cerambycidæ	*Eburia*	*quadrigeminata* Say	Bole	541	38	96	----	-----	-----	-----	462
	Neoclytus	*capræa* Say	Bole	543	36	95	----	-----	-----	-----	279
	Neoclytus	*erythrocephalus* Fab.	Bole	228	37	96	----	-----	-----	-----	71
Scarabæidæ	*Dynastes*	*tityus* Linn.	Leaves	551	32	89	28	-----	-----	-----	---------
Ptinidæ	*Lyctus*	?	Bole	-----	39	98	----	all	-----	[2]388	[3]296
Scolytidæ	*Hylesinus*	*aculeatus* Say	Bole	543	20	75	----	-----	[1]320	-----	288

[1] As *Meliobius*. [2] *L. striatus*. [3] *L. unipunctatus*.

Damage to Pinus spp. by Lepidoptera

Family	Genus	Species	Parts Suffering	Literary References												
				5th Rept. Ent. Com. U. S.	Ent. Bul. No. 48 U. S.	Ent. Bul. No. 53 U. S.	Ent. Bul. No. 37 U. S.	Ent. Bul. No. 32 U. S.	Ent. Bul. No. 21 U. S.	Ent. Bul. No. 7 U. S.	For Bul No. 22 U. S.	For Rpt No. 7 N. Y.	Ex. Sta. No. 56 W. Va.	Comstock's Man.	Ag. Yr. Bk. for 1907 U. S.	St. Mus. No. 8 N. Y.
ieridæ	*Neophasia*	*menapia* Feld.	Needles	762	28	84	21	----	17, 26	77	---	---	---	-----	159	----
phingidæ	*Lapara*	*bombycoides* Walk	Needles	-----	----	----	----	----	-----	----	---	---	---	-----	-----	----
	Lapara	*coniferarum* S & A	Needles	[1]768	----	----	----	----	-----	----	---	---	---	-----	-----	----
eratocampidæ	*Basilona*	*imperialis* Dru.	Needles	[2]646	28	85	----	----	-----	----	---	---	---	346	-----	677
rctiidæ	*Euschausia*	*argentata* Pack.	Needles	-----	29	85	----	----	-----	----	---	---	---	-----	-----	----
esiidæ	*Parharmonia*	*pini* Vrell.	Bole	[3]727	----	----	----	14	-----	----	[3]59	---	---	[3]261	-----	341
	Vespamima	*sequoia* Hy. Edw.	Bole (in sapl).	-----	----	----	----	14	-----	----	---	---	---	-----	-----	----
hycitidæ	*Pinipestis*	*zimmermanni* Grte	Twigs	844, 856	----	----	----	----	-----	----	59	501	---	236	-----	403
	?	?	Fruit	-----	33	90	----	----	-----	----	---	---	---	-----	-----	----
ortricidæ	*Evetria*	*comstockiana* Fern	Twigs	[4]743	----	----	----	----	-----	----	---	[4]503	---	-----	-----	407
	Evetria	*frustrana* Comst.	Twigs	[4]745, 753	----	----	----	----	-----	----	---	[4]501	[4]451	[4]243	-----	405
	Evetria	*rigidana* Fern.	Twigs	[4]754	----	----	----	----	-----	----	---	[4]503	---	-----	-----	407
	Enarmonia	*bracteatana* Fern.	Fruit	[5]788	----	----	----	----	-----	----	---	---	---	-----	-----	----
	Eulia	*politana* Haw.	Needles	[6]791	----	----	----	----	-----	----	---	---	[8]451	[9]245	-----	----
	?	?		-----	23	79	----	----	-----	----	---	---	---	-----	-----	----
elechiidæ	*Paralechia*	*pinifoliella* Cham.	Needles	[7]793	----	----	----	----	-----	----	---	[7]509	[7]451	[7]252	-----	----

[1]As *Ellema*. [2]As *Eacles*. [3]As *Harmonia*. [4]As *Retinia*. [5]As *Enarmonia*. [6]As *Tortrix*. [7]As *Gelechia*. [8]As *Lophoderes politanus*. [9]As *Lophoderus*.

Damage to Picea spp. by Lepidoptera

Family	Genus	Species	Parts Suffering	Literary References					
				5th Rept. Ent. Com. U. S.	Ent. Bul. No. 48 U. S.	Ent. Bul. No. 53 U. S.	Ent. Bul. No 37 U. S.	Ent. Bul. No. 21 U. S.	St. Mus. Mem. No. 8 N. Y.
Geometridæ	*Philedia*	*punctomacularia*‡	Needles	-----	----	----	22	18	---------
	?	?	Needles	-----	----	----	----	26, 18	---------
Phycitidæ	*Dioryctria*	*reniculella* Grote	Fruit	[1]854	[1]33	[1]90	----	----	---------
Tortricidæ	*Tortrix*	*fumiferana* Clem.	Twigs	830	----	----	----	----	416
Gelechiidæ	*Recurvaria*	*obliquestrigella* Clam	Twigs	[2]850	----	----	----	----	---------

[1]As *Pinipestis*. [2]As *Gelechia*. ‡Hulst.

Damage to Tsuga spp. by Lepidoptera

Family	Genus	Species	Parts Suffering	Literary References				
				5th Rept. Ent. Com U S.	Ent. Bul. No 37 U. S.	Ent. Bul No. 21 U. S	Ag. Yr. Bk. for 1907 U. S.	
Pieridæ	*Neophasia*	*menapia* Feld.	Needles	762	21	17, 26	159	

Damage to Sequoia spp. by Lepidoptera

Family	Genus	Species	Parts Suffering	Literary References		
				5th Rept Ent. Com. U. S	For. Bul No. 38 U. S.	
Sesiidæ	*Vespamima*	*sequoiæ* Hy. Edw.	Twigs	[1]922	32	

[1]*Bembecia*

Damage to Juniperus spp. by Lepidoptera

Family	Genus	Species	Parts Suffering	Literary References						
				5th Rept. Ent. Com. U. S	For. Bul. No. 31 U. S	Far Bul. No. 99 U. S.	Ent. Cir. No. 97 U. S.	Com-stock's Manual	Ag.Yr.Bk. for 1895 U. S	St. Mus. Mem. No. 8 N. Y.
Psychidæ	*Thyridopteryx*	*ephemeræformis** ‡	Needles	258	26	5	all	220	361	123

*A very general feeder but found most commonly on evergreens. ‡Haw.

Damage to Hicoria spp. by Lepidoptera

Family	Genus	Species	Parts Suffering	Literary References					
				5th Rept. Ent. Com. U. S.	Ent. Bul. No. 48 U. S.	Ent. Bul No. 53 U. S.	Comstock's Manual	St. Mus. Bul. No 110 N. Y.	St. Mus. Mem. No. 8 N. Y.
Sphingidæ	*Cressonia*	*juglandis* S. & A.	Leaves	-----	28	84	----	--------	518
Saturniidæ	*Telea*	*polyphemus* Cram.	Leaves	300	----	----	352	--------	526
Ceratocampidæ	*Basilona*	*imperialis* Dru.	Leaves	[1]646	28	85	346	--------	677
	Citheronia	*regalis* Fab.	Leaves	301, 331	28	85	346	--------	305
Arctiidæ	*Halisidota*	*caryæ* Harr	Leaves	[2]299	29	85	320	59	314
Notodontidæ	*Datana*	*integerrima* Dru.	Leaves	150	30	86	----	59	303
	Datana	*ministra* G. & R.	Leaves	476	30	86	265	--------	535
Tortricidæ	*Enarmonia*	*caryana* Fitch	Fruit	[3]326	[3]33	[3]90	----	--------	583

[1]As *Eacles*. [2]As *Halesidota*. [3]As *Grapholitha*.

Damage to Betula spp. by Lepidoptera

Family	Genus	Species	Parts Suffering	Literary References				
				5th Rept Ent. Com. U. S.	Ent. Bul. No. 48 U. S.	Ent. Bul. No. 53 U. S	Com-stock's Manual	St. Mus. Mem No. 8 N. Y.
Saturniidæ	*Telea*	*polyphemus* Cram	Leaves	400	28	84	352	526
Notodontidæ	*Datana*	*ministra* Dru.	Leaves	476	30	86	265	535

Damage to Castanea spp. by Lepidoptera

Family	Genus	Species	Parts Suffering	Literary References		
				5th Rept. Ent. Com. U. S.	Comstock's Manual	
Geometridæ	*Ennomos*	*magnarius* Guen.	Leaves	-----	278	
Hepialidæ	*Sthenopis*	*argenteomaculatus*‡	Leaves	[1]346	-----	

[1]As *Hepialis*. ‡Harr.

Damage to Quercus spp. by Lepidoptera

Family	Genus	Species	Parts Suffering	Literary References: 5th Rept. Ent Com. U. S.	Ent Bul No. 48 U. S.	Ent. Bul No. 53 U. S.	Geo. Rpt. for 1899 N. J.	For Rept No. 7 N. Y.	St. Mus. No. 103 N. Y.	Ex. Sta. No 35 W. Va.	Comstock's Man.	Far. Bul No. 264 U. S.	Ag. Yr Bk for 1907 U. S.	St. Mus. No. 53 N. Y.	Ins. Bul. No. 7 Ohio	St. Mus. No. 8 N. Y.
aturniidæ	*Hemileuca*	*maia* Dru.	Leaves	162	29	85	----	525	-----	----	342	---	-----	-----	---	310
	Telea	*polyphemus* Cram.	Leaves	400	28	84	----	----	-----	----	352	---	-----	-----	---	526
'eratocampidæ	*Anisota*	*senatoria* S. & A.	Leaves	124	28	85	----	524	-----	----	348	---	-----	-----	---	306
	Anisota	*stigma* Fab.	Leaves	125	28	85	----	----	-----	----	348	---	-----	-----	---	527
rctiidæ	*Halisidota*	*tessellaris* S. & A.	Leaves	265	29	85	----	----	-----	----	---	---	-----	-----	---	523
	Hyphantria	*textor* Harr.	Leaves	-----	29	86	----	----	-----	----	---	---	-----	-----	---	142
'octuidæ	*Catocala*	spp.	Leaves	174, 465 476	29 30	86 86	---- ----	---- ----	----- -----	---- ----	298 265	--- ---	----- -----	----- -----	--- ---	----
'otodontidæ	*Datana*	*ministra* Dru.	Leaves													538
	Datana	*angusii* G. & R.	Leaves	473	30	86	----	----	-----	----	265	---	-----	-----	---	535
	Symmerista	*albifrons* S. & A.	Leaves	[1]152	30	87	----	----	-----	----	[1]266	---	-----	-----	---	510
iparidæ	*Euproctis*	*chrysorrhea* Linn.	Leaves	-----	30	87	----	----	7	----	---	all	-----	-----	---	163
	Notolophus	*antiqua* Linn.	Leaves	[2]447	30	87	----	----	7	----	311	---	-----	-----	---	524
	**Porthetria*	*dispar* Linn.	Leaves	[3]138	30	----	----	----	14	----	312	---	153	-----	---	116
asiocampidæ	*Malacosoma*	*disstria* Hubn.	Leaves	[4]117	30	87	207	----	-----	----	[4]362	---	-----	-----	---	106
'ochilidiidæ	*Euclea*	*delphinii* Boisd.	Leaves	-----	31	89	----	----	-----	----	224	---	-----	-----	---	----
legalopygidæ	*Lagoa*	*crispata* Pack.	Leaves	139	31	88	----	----	-----	----	[6]218	---	-----	-----	---	529
'ossidæ	*Prionoxystus*	*robiniæ* Peck	Bole & Twigs	53	40	99	214	----	-----	299	222	---	-----	744	12	79
'ortricidæ	*Archips*	*fervidana* Clem.	Leaves	[5]193	31	89	----	----	-----	----	[5]245	---	-----	-----	---	530
	Tortrix	*quercifoliana* Fitch	Leaves	191	----	----	----	----	-----	----	---	---	-----	-----	---	542
lastobasidæ	*Holcocera*	*glandulella* Riley	Fruit	216	----	----	----	----	-----	----	---	---	-----	-----	---	----
'ineidæ	*Lithocolletes*	*hamadryella* Clem.	Leaves	-----	----	----	----	----	-----	----	250	---	-----	-----	---	532

[1]As *Edema*. [2]As *Orgyia*. [3]As *Ocneria*. [4]As *Clisiocampa*. [5]As *Cacœcia*. [6]As *Megalopyge*. *See Entire Forest Bulletin No. 265, U. S.

Damage to Ulmus spp. by Lepidoptera

Family	Genus	Species	Parts Suffering	Literary References: 5th Rept. Ent. Com. U. S.	Ent. Bul. No. 48 U. S.	Ent. Bul. No. 53 U. S.	Ent. Bul. No. 7 U. S.	Far. Bul. No 99 U. S.	For. Rept. No. 4 N. Y.	Comstock's Manual	Ag. Yr. Bk. for 1895 U. S.	St. Mus. Bul. No. 109 N. Y.	St. Mus. Bul. No. 53 N. Y.	St. Mus. Mem. No 8 N. Y.
Nymphalidæ	*Euvanessa*	*antiopa* Linn.	Leaves	[1]448	27	83	----	-----	----	403	-----	--------	--------	158
	Polygonia	*interrogationis* Fab	Leaves	-----	[4]27	83	48	-----	----	405	-----	--------	--------	544
Sphingidæ	*Ceratomia*	*amyntor* Geyer	Leaves	242	28	84	----	-----	----	------	-----	--------	--------	546
Arctiidæ	*Halisidota*	*maculata* Harr.	Leaves	[2]133	29	85	----	-----	----	------	-----	--------	--------	523
	Halisidota	*tesselaris* S. & A.	Leaves	[2]265	29	85	----	-----	----	------	-----	--------	--------	523
Noctuidæ	*Apatela*	*americana* Harr.	Leaves	397	29	86	----	-----	----	[5]307	-----	--------	--------	525
Liparidæ	*Hemerocampa*	*leucostigma* S. & A.	Leaves	[3]262	----	----	----	[3]12	[3]368	[6]310	[3]368	6	--------	132
Cossidæ	*Zeuzera*	*pyrina* Linn.	Bole & Twigs	-----	----	----	----	-----	380	------	-----	--------	745	75
Geometridæ	*Paleacrita*	*vernata* Peck	Leaves	230	31	88	----	-----	----	275	-----	--------	--------	547

[1]As *Vanessa*. [2]As *Halesidota*. [3]As *Orgyia*. [4]As *Grapta*. [5]As *Acronycta*. [6]As *Notolophus*.

Damage to Robinia spp. by Lepidoptera

Family	Genus	Species	Parts Suffering	Literary References											
				5th Rept. Ent. Com. U. S.	Ent. Bul. No. 48 U. S.	Ent. Bul. No. 53 U. S.	Far. Bul. No. 90 U. S.	Geol. Rept for 1899 N. J.	For. Rept No. 4 N. Y.	Com-stock's Man.	Ag. Yr. Bk. for 1895 U. S.	St. Mus. No. 100 N. Y.	St. Mus. No. 53 N. Y.	Ins. Bul. No. 7 Ohio	St. Mus. No. 8 N. Y.
Hesperidæ	*Epargyreus*	*tityrus* Fab.	Leaves	[1]365	28	84	----	-----	----	370	-----	----	----	27	556
Arctiidae	*Hyphantria*	*cunea* Dru.	Leaves	244	----	----	20	-----	----	----	375	----	----	41	----
Liparidæ	*Hemerocampa*	*leucostigma* S. & A.	Leaves	[2]262	----	----	[3]12	-----	[3]368	[3]310	[3]368	6	----	39	----
Cossidæ	*Prionoxystus*	*robiniæ* Peck.	Bole & Twigs	53	----	----	----	214	----	----	-----	----	744	12	70
	Zeuzera	*pyrina* Linn.	Branches	-----	----	----	----	-----	----	----	-----	----	----	36	----
Tortrycidæ	*Ecdytolopha*	*insiticiana* Zell.	Twigs	359	----	----	----	-----	----	----	-----	----	----	19	478

[1]As *Eudamus*. [2]As *Orgyia*. [3]As *Notolophus*.

Damage to Acer spp. by Lepidoptera

Family	Genus	Species	Parts Suffering	Literary References										
				5th Rept. Ent. Com. U. S.	Ent. Bul. No. 48 U. S.	Ent. Bul. No. 53 U. S.	Far. Bul. No. 99 U. S.	For. Rept. No. 4 N. Y.	Comstock's Manual	Ent. Bul No. 37 U. S.	Ag. Yr. Bk. for 1895 U. S.	St. Mus. Bul. No 109 N. Y.	St. Mus. Bul. No. 53 N. Y.	St. Mus Mem. No. 8 N. Y.
aturniidæ	*Automeris*	*io* Fab.	Leaves	[1]394	----	----	----	-----	351	----	-----	--------	--------	521
	Telea	*polyphemus* Cram.	Leaves	400	28	84	----	-----	------	----	-----	--------	--------	526
eratocampidæ	*Anisota*	*rubicunda* Fab.	Leaves	[2]392	----	----	----	-----	[2]349	----	-----	--------	--------	537
rctiidæ	*Halisidota*	*tessolaris* S. & A.	Leaves	[3]265	29	85	----	-----	------	----	-----	--------	--------	523
octuidæ	*Apatela*	*americana* Harr.	Leaves	397	29	86	----	-----	[6]301	----	-----	--------	--------	525
	Homoptera	*lunata* Dru.	Leaves	402	29	86	----	-----	296	----	-----	--------	--------	538
iparidæ	*Hemerocampa*	*leucostigma* S. & A.	Leaves	[4]262	----	----	[4]12	[7]368	[7]310	----	[4]368	6	--------	132
ossidæ	*Zeuzera*	*pyrina* Linn.	Bole & Twigs	-----	40	98	----	380	------	30	-----	--------	745	75
asiocampidæ	*Malacosoma*	*disstria* Hubn.	Leaves	[5]117	----	----	----	[5]374	------	----	-----	--------	--------	106
esiidæ	*Aegeria*	*acerni* Clem.	Bole	-----	----	----	----	[8]384	------	----	-----	--------	--------	56
ineidæ	*Incurvaria*	*acerifoliella* Fitch.	Leaves	408	----	----	----	-----	255	----	-----	--------	--------	541

[1]As *Hyperchiria*. [2]As *Dryocampa*. [3]As *Halesidota*. [4]As *Orgyia*. [5]As *Clisiocampa*. [6]As *Acronycta*. [7]As *Notolophus*. [8]As *Sesia*.

Damage to Tilia spp. by Lepidoptera

Family	Genus	Species	Parts Suffering	Literary References								
				5th Rept. Ent. Com. U. S.	Ent. Bul. No. 48 U. S.	Ent. Bul. No. 53 U. S.	Far. Bul. No. 99 U. S.	For. Rept. No. 4 N. Y.	Comstock's Manual	Ag. Yr. Bk. for 1895 U. S.	St. Mus. Bul. No. 109 N. Y.	St. Mus. Mem. No. 8 N. Y.
Saturniidæ	*Telea*	*polyphemus* Cram.	Leaves	400	28	84	----	-----	352	-----	--------	526
Notodontidæ	*Datana*	*ministra* Dru.	Leaves	476	30	86	----	-----	265	-----	--------	535
	Heterocampa	*bilineata* Pack.	Leaves	268	----	----	----	-----	[4]266	-----	--------	---------
Liparidæ	*Hemerocampa*	*leucostigma* S & A.	Leaves	[1]262 &c.	----	----	[1]12	[3]368	[3]310	[1]268	6	---------
Geometridæ	*Erannis*	*tiliaria* Harr.	Leaves	[2]475	----	----	----	-----	280	-----	--------	---------
Pyralidæ	*Pantographa*	*limata* G. & R.	Leaves	[2]477	----	----	----	-----	231	-----	--------	---------

[1]As *Orgyia*. [2]As *Hibernia*. [3]As *Notolophus*. [4]As *Seirodonta*.

Damage to Fraxinus spp. by Lepidoptera

Family	Genus	Species	Parts Suffering	Literary References						
				5th Rept. Ent. Com. U. S.	Ent. Bul. No. 48 U. S.	Ent. Bul No. 53 U. S.	Far. Bul. No. 99 U. S.	Comstock's Manual	Ag. Yr. Bk. for 1895 U. S.	St. Mus. Mem. No. 8 N. Y.
Sphingidæ	*Ceratomia*	*undulosa* Walk.	Leaves	-----	28	84	----	-----	-----	548
	Sphinx	*Kalmiæ* S. & A.	Leaves	-----	[1]28	84	----	-----	-----	548
Saturniidæ	*Callosamia*	*promethea* Dru.	Leaves	525	----	----	----	354	-----	557
Arctiidæ	*Hyphantria*	*cunea* Dru.	Leaves	244	----	----	20	321	375	---------

[1]As *Hyloicus*.

Damage to Catalpa spp. by Lepidoptera

Family	Genus	Species	Parts Suffering	Literary References		
				Ins. Bul. No. 7 Ohio	Ent. Cir. No. 96 U. S.	
Sphingidæ	*Ceratomia*	*catalpæ* Boisd.	Leaves	48	all	

Damage to Pinus spp. by Hymenoptera

Family	Genus	Species	Parts Suffering	Literary References						
				5th Rept. Ent. Com. U. S.	Ent. Bul. No. 48 U. S.	Ent. Bul. No. 53 U. S.	For. Bul. No. 22 U. S.	For. Rept. No. 7 N. Y.	Ex. Sta. Bul. No. 56 W. Va.	St. Mus. Mem. No. 8 N. Y.
Tenthredinidæ	*Lophyrus*	*abbotii* Leach	Needles	755	32	89	60	-----	425	[1]414
	Lophyrus	*lecontei* Fitch	Needles	758	----	----	----	508	---------	413
	Lyda	?	Needles	760	----	----	----	-----	---------	---------
Siricidæ	*Paururus*	*hopkinsi* Ashm.	Bole	-----	40	99	----	-----	---------	---------
	Paururus	*pinicola* Ashm.	Bole	-----	40	99	----	-----	---------	---------

[1]As *L. pini-rigidæ*.

Damage to Larix spp. by Hymenoptera

Family	Genus	Species	Parts Suffering	Literary References					
				5th Rept. Ent. Com U. S.	Ent. Bul. No. 48 U. S.	Ent. Bul. No. 53 U. S.	Ratzeburg Vol III	Ag. Yr. Bk. for 1907 U. S	St. Mus. Mem. No. 8 N. Y.
Tenthredinidæ	*Lygæonematus*	*erichsonii* Hart	Needles	879 [1]	[1]32	[1]89	[2]121	153	418

[1]As *Nematus* [2]As *Tenthredo*.

Damage to Picea spp. by Hymenoptera

Family	Genus	Species	Parts Suffering	Literary References: 5th Rept Ent. Com. U. S.	Ent. Bul No. 48 U. S.	Ent. Bul. No. 53 U. S.	Ex. Sta. Bul. No. 56 W. Va.	Comstock's Manual
Tenthredinidæ	*Nematus*	*integer* Say	Needles	838	----	----	--------	-----
Formicidæ	*Camponotus*	*pennsylvanicus* ‡	Bole	-----	----	----	431	635, 640
Siricidæ	*Urocerus*	*abdominalis* Harr.	Bole	733	40	99	425	-----
	Urocerus	*albicornis* Fab	Bole	733	40	99	--------	-----
	Urocerus	*flavipennis* Kby	Bole	-----	40	99	--------	-----

‡DeG.

Damage to Populus spp. by Hymenoptera

Family	Genus	Species	Parts Suffering	Literary References	
				For. Bul. No. 46 U. S.	St. Mus. Mem. No. 8 N. Y.
Tenthredinidæ	*Janus*	*integer* Nort.	Twigs	68	302
	Pteronus	*ventralis* Say	Leaves	70	322

Damage to Alnus glutinosa by Hymenoptera

Family	Genus	Species	Parts Suffering	Literary References
				Ex. Sta. Bul. No. 233 Cornell
Tenthredinidæ	*Kaliosphinga*	*dohrnii* Tischb.	Leaves	58

Damage to Quercus spp. by Hymenoptera

Family	Genus	Species	Parts Suffering	Literary References							
				5th Rept. Ent. Com. U. S.	Ent. Bul. No. 48 U. S.	Ent. Bul. No. 53 U. S.	For. Rept. No. 7 N. Y.	For. Rept. No. 4 N. Y.	Comstock's Manual	Guide Leaflet No. 16 A. M. N. H	St. Mus. Mem. No. 8 N. Y.
Cynipidæ	*Cynips, etc.*	spp. (very many)	Lvs. Tws. Frt	104	----	----	[1]530	-----	618	10-22	618
Tenthredinidæ	*Selandria*	*diluta* Cress.	Leaves	206	----	----	-----	-----	----	---------	---------
Siricidæ	*Tremex*	*columba* Linn.	Bole	379	40	99	-----	389	615	---------	61

[1]*Biorhiza forticornis* Walsh.

Damage to Ulmus spp. by Hymenoptera

Family	Genus	Species	Parts Suffering	Literary References: Ent. Bul. No. 48 U. S.	Ent. Bul. No. 53 U. S.	Far. Bul. No. 46 U. S.	For. Rept No. 7 N. Y.	Comstock's Manual	Ex. Sta. Bul. No. 233 Cornell	St. Mus. Mem. No. 8 N. Y.
Formicidæ	*Camponotus*	*herculeanus* Linn.	Bole	----	----	-----	522	----	--------	90
Tenthredinidæ	*Cimbex*	*americana* Leach	Leaves	32	89	72	-----	612	--------	155
	Kaliosphinga	*ulmi* Sund.	Leaves	----	----	-----	-----	----	49	162

F

Damage to Acer spp. by Hymenoptera

Family	Genus	Species	Parts Suffering	Literary References					
				5th Rept. Ent. Com. U. S.	Ent. Bul. No. 48 U. S.	Ent. Bul. No. 53 U. S.	For. Rept No. 4 N. Y.	Comstock's Manual	St. Mus. Mem. No. 8 N. Y.
Siricidæ	*Tremex*	*columba* Linn	Bole	379	40	99	389	615	61

Damage to Pinus spp. by Diptera

Family	Genus	Species	Parts Suffering	Literary References						
				5th Rept. Ent. Com. U. S.	Ent. Bul. No. 48 U. S.	Ent. Bul. No. 53 U. S.	For. Rept. No. 7 N. Y.	Ex. Sta. Bul. No. 56 W. Va.	Com-stock's Manual	St. Mus. Mem. No. 8 U. S.
Cecidomyiidæ	*Cecidomyia*	*pinirigidæ* Pack	Needles	[1]798	----	----	[1]510	[1]449, 451	-----	423
	Cecidomyia	*resinicola* O. S	Twigs	[1]797	----	----	[1]505	--------	[1]447	410
	?	?	Twigs	-----	23	78	-----	--------	-----	---------

[1]As *Diplosis*.

Damage to Hicoria spp., by Diptera

Family	Genus	Species	Parts Suffering	Literary References: G'de L'flet No 16 A. M. N. H.
Cecidomyiidæ	*Cecidomyia*	*caryæcola* O. S.	Leaves	27
	Cecidomyia	*holotricha* O. S.	Leaves	26
	Cecidomyia	*tubicola* O. S.	Leaves	27

Damage to Quercus spp., by Diptera

Family	Genus	Species	Parts Suffering	Literary References: 5th Rept Ent. Com. U. S	Literary References: G'de L'flet No. 16 A. M. N. H.
Cecidomyiidæ	*Cecidomyia*	*niveipila* O. S.	Leaves	-----	31
	Cecidomyia	*pilulæ* Walsh	Leaves	206	30
	Cecidomyia	*poculum* O. S.	Leaves	-----	30

Damage to Liriodendron spp. by Diptera

Family	Genus	Species	Parts Suffering	Literary References: G'de L'flet No. 16 A. M. N. H.
Cecidomyiidæ	*Cecidomyia*	*liriodendri* O. S.	Leaves	25
	Cecidomyia	*tulipifera* O. S.	Leaves	25

Damage to Cornus florida by Diptera

Family	Genus	Species	Parts Suffering	Literary References: G'de L'flet No 16 A. M. N. H.
Cecidomyiidæ	*Cecidomyia*	*clavula* Beuten	Twigs	29

Damage to Acer spp. by Diptera

Family	Genus	Species	Parts Suffering	Literary References: 5th Rept Ent. Com U. S	Literary References: G'de L'flet No. 16 A. M. N. H.
Mycetophilidæ	*Sciara*	*ocellata* O. S.	Leaves	411	33

Damage to Pinus spp. by Hemiptera

Family	Genus	Species	Parts Suffering	Literary References: 5th Rept. Ent. Com. U. S.	For. Bul. No. 22 U. S.	For. Bul. No. 7 N. Y.	Ex. Sta. Bul. No. 56 W. Va.	Comstock's Manual	St. Mus. Bul. No. 53 N. Y.	St. Mus. Mem. No. 8 N. Y.
Aphididæ	*Chermes*	*pinicorticis* Fitch	Twigs	810	----	505	--------	----	749	192
	Chermes	*strobi* Hart	Bole & Twigs	-----	----	----	--------	----	--------	---------
	Lachnus	*strobi* Fitch	Needles	803	----	----	--------	----	--------	---------
Coccidæ	*Chionaspis**	*pinifoliæ* Fitch	Needles	805	61	511	452	172	--------	229
	Lecanium	?	Twigs	-----	----	----	452	----	--------	---------
	Rhizococcus	?	Twigs	-----	----	----	452	----	--------	---------
Cercopidæ	*Aphrophora*	*paralella* Say	Twigs	741	----	----	452	----	--------	---------

*Formerly *Mytilaspis*.

Damage to Picea spp. by Hemiptera

Family	Genus	Species	Parts Suffering	Literary References: 5th Rept. Ent. Com. U. S.	Ent. Bul. No. 48 U. S.	Ent. Bul. No. 53 U. S.	Ex. Sta. Bul. No. 56 W. Va.	St. Mus. Mem. No. 8 U. S.
Aphididæ	*Chermes*	*abietis* Linn.	Twigs	[1]853	----	----	452	189
	Chermes	*sibiricus* Chold.	Twigs	-----	23	79	--------	---------
Coccidæ	*Rhizococcus*	?	Twigs	-----	----	----	452	---------

[1]As *Lachnus*.

Damage to Juglans spp. by Hemiptera

Family	Genus	Species	Parts Suffering	Literary References	
				Geol. Rept. for 1899 N. J.	
Coccidæ	*Mytilaspis*	?	Twigs	210	

Damage to Hicoria spp. by Hemiptera

Family	Genus	Species	Parts Suffering	Literary References		
				Geol. Rept. for 1899 N. J.	Guide Leaflet No. 16 A. M. N. H.	St. Mus. Mem. No. 8 N. Y.
Aphididæ	*Phylloxera*	*caryæcaulis* Fitch.	Lvs. & Twigs	209	38	331
Coccidæ	*Lecanium*	sp.	Twigs	210	---------	---------

Damage to Alnus spp. by Hemiptera

Family	Genus	Species	Parts Suffering	Literary References		
				5th Rept. Ent. Com. U. S.	Comstock's Manual	St. Mus. Mem. No. 8 N. Y.
Aphididæ	*Pemphigus*	*tessellatus* Fitch	Lvs. & Twigs	[1]637	[1]161	195

[1]As *Schizoneura tessellata.*

Damage to Fagus spp. by Hemiptera

Family	Genus	Species	Parts Suffering	Literary References	
				Comstock's Manual	
Aphididæ	*Schizoneura*	*imbricator* Fitch	Lvs. & Twigs	161	

Damage to Quercus spp. by Hemiptera

Family	Genus	Species	Parts Suffering	Literary References						
				Ent Bul. No. 48 U. S.	Ent. Bul. No. 53 U. S.	Ent. Bul. No. 14 U. S.	Ent. Bul. No 71 U. S.	Com-stock's Manual	St. Mus. Bul. No. 53 N. Y.	St. Mus. Mem. No. 8 N. Y.
Cicadidæ	**Tibicen*	*septendecim* Linn.	Twigs	33	91	all	all	150	231	----------
Coccidæ	*Kermes*	?	Leaves	----	----	----	----	168	----------	----------
	Asterolecanium	*variolosum* Ratz.	Twigs	----	----	----	----	----	746	329
	***Aspidiotus*	*perniciosus* Comst.	Bole & Twigs	----	----	----	----	----	216	----------

*Formerly *Cicada*. **The Literature on this species is voluminous, but principally deals with its occurrence on fruit trees.

Damage to Ulmus spp. by Hemiptera

Family	Genus	Species	Parts Suffering	Literary References	
				St. Mus. Mem. No. 8 N. Y.	
Aphididæ	*Callipterus*	*ulmifolii* Monell	Leaves	176	
	Schizoneura	*americana* Riley	Leaves	177	
	Colopha	*ulmicola* Fitch	Leaves	186	
Coccidæ	*Chionaspis*	*americana* Johns	Bole & Twigs	207	
	Gossyparia	*spuria* Mod.	Bole & Twigs	203	

Damage to Liriodendron spp. by Hemiptera

Family	Genus	Species	Parts Suffering	Literary References		
				Geol. Rept. for 1899 N. J.	St. Mus. Mem. No. 8 N. Y.	
Coccidæ	*Eulecanium*	*tulipiferæ* Cook	Twigs	[1]210	208	

[1]As *Lecanium*.

Damage to Acer spp. by Hemiptera

FAMILY	GENUS	SPECIES	PARTS SUFFERING	LITERARY REFERENCES								
				5th Rept. Ent. Com. U. S.	Ent. Bul. No. 48 U. S.	Ent. Bul. No. 53 U. S.	Ent. Bul. No. 14 U. S.	Ent. Bul. No. 71 U. S.	For. Rept. No. 4 N. Y.	Com-stock's Manual	St. Mus. Bul. No. 53 N. Y.	St. Mus. Mem. No. 8 N. Y.
Cicadidæ	*Tibicen**	*septendecim* Linn.	Twigs	95	33	91	all	all	-----	150	--------	231
Coccidæ	*Aspidiotus*	*tenebricosus* Comst.	Twigs	417	33	91	----	----	-----	----	--------	---------
	Pulvinaria	*innumerabilis* †	Twigs	412	33	91	----	----	393	169	--------	196
	Lecanium	*nigrofasciatum* Prg.	Limbs	-----	----	----	----	----	-----	----	748	[1]200
	Pseudococcus	*aceris* Geoff.	Bole	-----	----	----	----	----	-----	----	749	---------
	Phenacoccus	*acericola* King.	Leaves	-----	----	----	----	----	-----	----	--------	182
	Pulvinaria	*acericola* W. & R.	Leaves	-----	----	----	----	----	-----	----	--------	179
Aphididæ	*Chaitophorus*?	*aceris* Linn.	Leaves	-----	----	----	----	----	-----	----	--------	174
	Drepanosiphum	*acerifolii* Thos.	Leaves	-----	----	----	----	----	-----	----	--------	175

*Formerly *Cicada*. †Rathy [1]As *Eulecanium*.

Damage to Various Woods by Isoptera

Family	Genus	Species	Parts Suffering	Literary References		
				Ag Yr.Bk. for 1904 U. S.	St. Mus. Mem. No. 8 N. Y.	
Termitidæ	*Leucotermes*	*flavipes* Koll.	seas'n'd wood	[1]389	[1]87	

[1]As *Termes*.

Damage to Various Conifers by Orthoptera

Family	Genus	Species	Parts Suffering	Literary References		
				For. Rept. No. 7 N. Y.	Comstock's Manual	
Gryllidæ	*Gryllotalpa*	*borealis Burm.*	Rts. nurse'ies	-----	117	
	Gryllus	spp.	Rts. nurse'ies	-----	117	
	Oecanthus	*pini* Beut.	Leaves	512	118	

Damage to Various Broad-Leaved Trees by Orthoptera

Family	Genus	Species	Parts Suffering	Literary References					
				5th Rept. Ent. Com. U. S.	Ent. Bul. No. 48 U. S.	Ent. Bul. No. 53 U. S.	For. Rept 1901-02 Penn.	Com-stock's Manual	St. Mus. Mem No. 8 N. Y.
Phasmidæ	*Diapheromera*	*femorata* Say	Lvs. & Twigs	317	32	89	46	108	533
Locustidæ	*Microcentrum*	*laurifolium* Linn.	Leaves	-----	32	89	-----	[1]113	---------

[1] As *M. retinervis*.

CHAPTER III: PROTECTION AGAINST PLANTS.

Par. 6. Protection Against Weeds.

Weeds are plants, herbaceous or lignaceous in character, the presence of which in the woods is financially undesirable.

A. Influencing Factors.

I. A plant may appear as a weed in one locality whilst it is useful in another. Kalmia, e. g., is useful on steep slopes by holding the soil; whilst it is harmful on areas in regeneration. Grasses and herbaceous weeds are valuable on forest pastures; they may interfere, however, with natural regeneration from seeds.

II. A plant may be considered as a weed at a certain stage of certain sylvicultural operations. This is the case with black gum, witch hazel, box elder, halesia which forms a superstructure interfering with the regeneration of yellow poplar, chestnut, and yellow pine. On the other hand, these same species may be valuable as an undergrowth or as a companion growth with yellow poplar, chestnut, pine and oak after the thicket stage.

III. A plant of a usually valuable kind may be classed as a weed when it is hopelessly deformed; e g , decrepit, hollow, burned chestnuts; fire shoots of hickory and oak.

Thus the forester might distinguish between "absolute weeds," which are always damaging, and "relative weeds," which are damaging only under a given set of conditions.

B. Most weeds injure the forest only indirectly. Direct damage is done by parasitic weeds, in rare cases. The most note-worthy cases of indirect injury are the following:

I. Smilax, grapevine, blackberry interfere with the transportation of wood goods and with the ease of access to the woods.

II. Sedge grass, heather, blueberry form a matting through which water or air cannot pass.

III. The mineral fertility of the soil is absorbed by the weeds (especially the fruiting weeds) competing with the trees for a food supply.

IV. The weeds, notably those produced after fires, interfere with the natural regeneration of the best species of the forest; they prevent, through dense shade, the lignification of the valuable seedlings during summer. Instances are: Chinquapin and gum in the case of yellow pine regeneration at Biltmore; witch hazel, dogwood in yellow poplar regeneration in Pisgah forest; black jack oak in long leaf pine forests.

V. Some weeds distort and oppress the seedlings and saplings after climbing to their tops. Grapevine on yellow poplar; *Convolvulus* on many tree seedlings. In tropical countries, the tree climbers (sometimes parasitic) are particularly troublesome, notably in felling trees.

VI. Certain weed species (notably *Ericaceæ*) produce, through their leaf fall, an unfavorable, dusty humus.

VII. Weeds harbor and hide mice and damaging insects.

VIII. Dead weeds increase the danger of fires, especially in the spring.

IX. The dead mould spread on the ground by many weeds prevents the germinating seed of valuable species from sending its rootlets into the mineral soil.

X. Certain weeds play an important part in the pathology of the trees, the weeds acting as hosts for the second generation of certain fungi.

C. Means of Protection.

I. Preventive measures.

a. Maintain a complete cover overhead—a pious wish in the primeval forests.

b. Underplant light demanding species with shade bearers at a time at which the leaf canopy overhead, through friction of crown against crown, becomes excessively open—another pious wish under the present conditions confronting American silviculture.

c. Work towards immediate reforestation after making a clean sweep of the old crop.

d. Insist on thorough protection against ground fires which, above all, foster the growth of weeds and are injurious to the nobility amongst the forest species. Kalmia, chinquapin, alder, soft maple, gum, halesia obtain the upper hand in the forest through fires. On fertile soil the growth of annual and biennial weeds after fires is especially luxuriant. In the Adirondacks, the reforestation of fire-swept tracts is handicapped by the excessive growth of forest weeds.

e. Admit for pasture cattle, hogs, sheep and goats, thus checking at the same time the danger from fires.

II. Restrictive Measures.

a. Cut (with a mowing scythe) herbaceous weeds before the seed ripens.

b. In forest plantations, cultivate the rows of plants, or raise farm crops together with seedlings.

c. Plow abandoned fields thorouglhy before reforestation.

d. Crush blackberry briars; decapitate ferns; skin thorns; deaden gum, dogwood, maple, beech; remove the bark for 2 ft. above the stump on cottonwoods to prevent the growth of root suckers.

e. Cover the stumps of undesirable hardwoods with dirt or brush; poison the stumps; peel the stumps down into the roots, set fire to brush heaps massed upon such stumps in coppice woods.

D. Weed Species

I. Andromeda, huckleberry, etc., are expelled by the continued use of a briar scythe, preferably in early August. Valuable seedlings are planted on reversed sods when placed in thickets formed by the above species.

II. Kalmia and Rhododendron may be checked by burning. They sprout luxuriantly after such burning. They do not catch up, however, with the more rapid development of the seedlings planted at the same time. In other cases, it is better to allow ivy and laurel to grow unharmed. The stems when over 4″ in diameter can be deadened readily.

III. Chinquapin may be deadened with crushing tongs in spring.

IV. Dogwood may be deadened. Dogwood sprouts grow vigorously from the stumps; hence it will not suffice to cut the dogwood with an axe.

V. Large trees of black gum are skinned or deadened. It is impossible to get rid of small shoots.

VI. Hazel, Vaccinium and Azalea on mountain pastures can be checked by the use of a colter, by repeated mowings or, possibly, by pasturing goats

VII. Blackberry is expelled by crushing its shoots or by skinning them between two pieces of timber.

VIII. Ferns should be decapitated in early spring.

IX. Climbers (*Clematis*, *Vitis*, *Ampelopsis* and others) are checked by cutting close to the ground.

Par. 7. Protection Against Fungi.

The diseases of our American trees caused by fungi have been studied by Dr. Hermann von Schrenk, of the Shaw School of Botany. Still, it must be admitted that our knowledge of the diseases of trees induced by cryptogamic parasites is deficient or inadequate. In the forest, obviously, the present conditions confronting forestry do not allow of "tree doctoring." Nurseries and young plantations in which fungi may cause enormous damage are practically absent from our forests. Fungi directly causing the death of trees, of over 12 inches d.b.h., are practically unknown.

Saplings and poles killed by fungi die from below, whilst those killed by insects die from above.

A. Effect of Fungus Infection.

Observations in the United States are at hand only with reference to fungi of a technically damaging character.

Such fungi may cause:—

I. Disintegration of lignin, leaving the shining white fibres of cellulose untouched.

II. Disintegration of cellulose leaving a brittle brown mass resembling charcoal.

III. Disintegration of entire cell walls, leaving a hole or holes.

IV. Liquification of the rosin incrustating the heartwood, in which case the rosin exudes at branch holes where it solidifies by oxidation, forming knots, galls or streaks of rosin.

B. Parts of Tree Infected; and Methods of Infection.

Fungi may attack the heartwood, or the sapwood, or both heartwood and sapwood. Heartwood fungi (which never kill a tree directly) enter through insect mines; through axe scars; through branch stubs having heartwood, or through tops broken off by snow, by sleet, by falling neighbors or by storm. For the latter reason, diseased timber prevails frequently along wind swept ridges and shores.

Sapwood fungi may use the same channels of access, or may enter the wood through lightning streaks and through fire clefts. Sapwood resists the attack of fungi much better than heartwood as long as the tree lives. The sapwood is the life zone of the tree in which it defends itself readily, by thickening its cell walls or by cell wall incrustations, or by forming cork against the spread of hyphæ.

In dead trees, on the other hand, sapwood decomposes much more readily than heartwood owing to the absence of incrustating substances and owing to the presence of more moisture, more starch and more albumen.

The insects co-operate with the fungi to an unknown extent. Corky bark being fungus-proof, many spores enter the galleries of boring insects either carried by the wind or carried in the "fur" of borers and enemies of borers It might be stated that the insects distribute spores in the same manner in which the birds or the rodents distribute seeds. A particularly interesting case is that of "Ambrosia," a fungus supposed to be raised by the Ambrosia beetles. Cyllene robiniæ makes possible the inroads of Polyporus rimosus. Discoloration of the sapwood coincides with the attacks of Dendroctonus frontalis and follows the "steamships" in oak lumber. A fungus-lawn is found in the mines of Lymexylon.

Infection is performed

(a) most frequently by spores,

1. in dew or rain (notably—the lower fungi);

2. by wind (notably—the higher fungi);

3. by insects (rarely, after Tubeuf);

4. by forcible ejection of spores from sporocarps, asci and sporangia

(b) more rarely by mycelium,

1. notably when the mycelium lives in the earth, or rather in the roots (*Trametes radiciperda, Agaricus melleus* "(Rhizomorphs)";

2. also above ground, the mycelium spreading from plant to plant (*Trichosphæria, Herpotrichia*).

Many fungi appear immediately after the affection of the tree by other detrimental influences (e. g. after insects, fire, storm, drought), so that it is possible to decide upon the immediate cause of damage inflicted only by the test of artificial infection. The fungi found present upon a dead tree can never be considered, *eo ipso*, as tree killers.

In many cases the mycelium of the tree killer has disappeared when the tree is dead; and only sporocarps may be still present. Many parasites on the other hand develop sporocarps only saprophytically on a dead substratum.

Certain timber fungi stop work at once when the tree is cut, e. g., the yellow rot fungus of black locust and the peckiness fungus of bald cypress. The progress of decay, in such cases, ends with the death of the tree.

The speed at which a fungus disease spreads from a given point of attack is entirely unknown. This speed is very fast in the case of saprophytes working in dead sapwood; it is probably very slow in the case of parasitic fungi attacking the heartwood of grown trees.

The tales of cruisers to the effect that a tract will "become punky in ten to fifteen years" do not seem to deserve any credit.

An old tree is, *ceteris paribus*, more readily affected, and more apt to be found affected by disease, than a young one.

C. Beneficial Fungi.

The symbiosis of certain fungi with certain trees (discovered by Frank) seems to be beneficial to both; possibly essential to both.

Many of our trees and shrubs are dependent upon certain fungi, at least for such foods as are derived from humus. These fungi consist of delicate, cobwebby threads such as are seen on mouldy bread. These threads spread through the soil and either enter the outer cells of the root or simply form a mantle (Mycorrhiza) about the root. The fungi live upon decaying animal and plant matter, and transfer a portion of this food to the root and doubtless secure in return certain benefits from the root. This mutual helpful relationship of two plants is termed *commensalism.*

The majority of our heaths, evergreens, poplars, willows, beeches and oaks have become dependent upon these fungi and do not thrive in soils where the fungi are not found.

Some herbaceous plants, like the Indian-pipe, have become entirely dependent upon these fungi for food and have, as a consequence, lost all their chlorophyll.

This field of forest ecological study is practically untouched, though it will form the basis of future silviculture. Certain fungi might be used, technologically, for the preparation of pure cellulose.

D. Signs of disease.

The signs of disease are visible only on a tree, usually, when it is too late to save the patient.

These signs are:—

A. Hypertrophical swellings, f i, knots on Spanish oak and tumors on yellow pine at Biltmore.

B. Exudations of rosin in galls or in seams.

C. Appearance of sporophores, which are rare in some species, but are frequently seen on diseased red oak, locust, and ash. When decaying holes appear on a tree, the forester is apt to find the whole tree diseased. Yellow poplar trees are sound within one foot, and white oak logs are sound within two feet from the actual end of a cavity.

The tree weeds, e. g., Halesia (*Mohrodendron*), gum and calmia, might be exterminated in days to come with the help of their fungus enemies.

E. Synopsis of the orders of damaging fungi.

I. Order ***Phycomycetes***. Family ***Peronosporeæ***.

The mycelium is unicellular. The propagation is effected by numerous branching hyphæ forming at their tips little sacs or sporangia in clusters or chains (conidia). These are carried by wind to other plants where they germinate at once, forming a tube that penetrates the leaf. If the leaf is wet, the contents of the sporangia break up into a number of zoospores which develop the characteristic hyphæ of the fungi. Sexual reproduction occurs in most species and consists of a gametangia cut off from the ends of the hyphæ and fertilized by male gametes developed on branches (antheridia) of the gametangia bearing hyphæ. The resulting thick walled gametospore tides the fungus over winter.

American representatives are not fully known. Some bad nursery fungi belong to this family (notably ***Phytophtora omnivora***).

II. Order ***Ascomycetes***.

1st. Family—*Pyrenomycetes*.

Flask-shaped frutifications (perithecia) are characteristic of this family. Within the perithecia, which are open at the top (angiocarpous), occur numerous asci, each containing eight spores. Preceeding the formation of perithecia, conidiospores are usually formed which are especially efficacious in disseminating the fungi. Examples: *Nectria* on maple and beech.

2nd. Family—*Discomycetes*.

Distinguished by open gymnocarpous apothecia (cup-shaped receptacles, bearing freely exposed asci).

The *Discomycetes* are unimportant for the American forester, none being observed as damaging our trees. *Rhytisma acerinum* frequently forms large black incrustations of pseudo-parenchyma on the leaves of maple, conidia developing in the summer and mature apothecia in the succeeding spring. The most important representative of this family in Europe is *Peziza*.

III. Order *Basidiomycetes*.

Spores carried on basidia of definite shape and size, and bearing a fixed number of spores.

1st. Family—*Uredineæ*.

All are injurious parasites, the mycelium being in the intercellular spaces of the tissues (particularly in the leaves) of higher plants. These fungi change their hostplants, showing a double generation, and develop several kinds of asexual spores, according to the season and to the host; æcidiospores and pycnoconidia in spring; uredospores in summer; teleutospores in autumn, which in the following spring develop basidiospores. The mycelium from the basidiospores enters the first host and develops the æcidium stage (formerly the genus *Aecidium*) with æcidia and pycnidia. The next stage on a different host develops the uredospores (formerly genus *Uredo*), and in autumn the thick walled teleutospores.

2nd. Family—*Hymenomycetes*.

Basidia imbedded in a common hymenium which clothes, in *Agaricaceæ*, a series of radial lamellæ on the under side of the pileus, and in *Polyporaceæ* and *Boletaceæ*, the inner surface of pores.

In a few genera no distinctive fructifications are formed (*Exobasidium vaccinii*, parasitic and causing hypertrophy on *Ericaceæ*).

Another arrangement of the orders and families of fungi might be made with reference to pathogeny:

a. The groups

Uredineæ *Ustilagineæ* (so-called "Smuts") *Peronosporeæ* *Exoasceæ* (witch broom)	contain parasites only, so that no proof of parasitism is required.

b. The groups *Pyrenomycetes* *Discomycetes* *Hymenomycetes* *Myxomycetes* And several groups of lower fungi and bacteria.	contain parasites as well as saprophytes so that proof of parasitism is required.

This proof is obtained by artificial infection only.

Infection reveals,—

(1) parasitic nature of a fungus,
(2) exact species of fungus,
(3) relationship of heterœcious *Uredineæ* and their host plants (uredinal, telial and æcidial stages),
(4) various forms of reproductive organs,
(5) conditions favorable to attacks.

The fungi might be further divided into two large groups, namely:

(a) Physiologically obnoxious species (tree killers and tree deformers) belonging to the orders *Phycomycetes* and *Ascomycetes* and to the family *Uredineæ* of the order *Basidiomycetes.*

(b) Technically obnoxious species (wood disintegrators) belonging notably to the family *Hymenomycetes;* this group may be sub-divided into fungi living on dead trees (Saprophytes) and fungi living on live trees (Parasites).

Group (a) is of greatest importance in Germany and France, whilst group (b) is of greatest importance in the United States.

F. According to parts attacked, the forest fungi might be subdivided as follows:

I. Nursery fungi and plantation fungi.
II. Root fungi in saplings and poles.
III. Leaf and twig fungi. (Bulletin Bureau of Plant Industry No. 149, page 18).
IV. Fungi causing hypertrophical formations (witch brooms).
V. Fungi discoloring lumber or timber.
VI. Fungi destroying the cambium and the sapwood of standing trees or poles.

VII. Fungi destroying the sapwood of dead trees and of logs.

VIII. Fungi destroying the heartwood in living trees.

IX. Fungi destroying timber, ties, poles and posts after manufacture and whilst in use.

G. Fungus species worthy of note which are physiologically obnoxious.

I. *Agaricus melleus* (honey fungus) is a champignon attacking and killing conifers four to fifteen years old. White pine suffers very badly. The disease spreads underground through the so-called rhizomorpha (strong threads of mycelium). The soil at the basis of affected plants is charged with exuded rosin. Comp. Bull. Plant Industry, No. 149, page 23.

II. *Aecidium pini* attacks the needles and the young bark of pine saplings. The spores enter by a wound and the spread of the mycelium in the cambium causes hypertrophical formations, especially on the main stem. The teleutosporous generation has a Senecio species for its host (*Coleosporium senecionis*).

III. *Peridermium cerebrum* (family *Uredineæ*) kills two year old lodgepole pines as well as other pines. (Agric. Year Book 1900, p. 200).

IV. *Peridermium strobi*, known as the blister of the white pine, has *Pinus cembra* for its original host. Whilst it does not injure this species seriously, its attacks are deadly to our white pine during its juvenile stage. In old trees well protected by heavy bark, the tops and branches alone are affected. The disease is frequent abroad; and stringent measures should prevent it from entering into the United States. The uredal form of the fungus (*Cronartium ribicolum*) forms blotches on the leaves of the currant (*Ribes*). Compare Quarterly Journal of Forestry, July, 1909, p. 232.

V. A *Gymnosporangium* causes the "Cedar apples" of red cedar; see Bull. 21, Div. of Pathology, p. 8. For. Bull. 31 (Red Cedar) p. 25.

VI. *Hysterium pinastri* causes the shedding disease dreaded in nurseries. Pine seedlings up to four years old drop the needles of a sudden in spring. White pine is little affected; strong seedlings are immune. The disease spreads through old needles on which the fungus lives saprophytically. Not observed in America so far.

VII. *Diaporthe parasitica* (discovered by Dr. Murrill) is the worst treekilling disease yet described in the United States. It tends to exterminate the chestnut trees from New York to Virginia, and is spreading southward. Entering the cambial layers of the tree and notably those of its branches without the requirement of preceding wounds, the mycelium actually "girdles" the living trees (W. A. Murrill, in Jour. N. Y. Bot. Garden 7: 143-153; Bull. No. 149, Bureau of Plant Industry, p. 22).

VIII. *Hypoderma strobicola* is the "needle blight" of the white pine and appears to be a dangerous parasite on *Pinus Strobus*. Compare Tubeuf's "Diseases of Plants," english edition by W. G. Smith, p. 233. Tubeuf claims that the disease may devastate whole tracts of forests. A disease of the white pine similar to that described by Tubeuf has been reported from Massachusetts (various articles in Woodland and Roadside), from Western North Carolina and from eastern Tennessee, and is being studied by the pathological divisions of the U. S. Dept. of Agriculture. Compare Circular No. 35, Bureau of Plant Industry.

IX. "Damping-off" is a disease of seedlings soon after germination dreaded by all nurserymen, and decimating many natural regenerations (birch!). The fungi causing the disease are undescribed.

H. Fungus species worthy of note which are technically obnoxious.

The genus *Polyporus* (including *Trametes*, *Fomes*, *Boletus*, *Polystictus*, and *Dædalea*) is responsible for the decomposition of heartwood in living trees frequently brought about by the help of an enzym.

Overaged timber is almost invariably attacked by *Polyporus*. The sporophores may appear in branch holes or scars, and are, although the disease might be common, rare in many species.

Most noteworthy are the following Polypori:—

I. *Polyporus annosus* (or *Trametes radiciperda*), a root fungus of conifers, attacks pole woods. Sporophores under ground in roots. Wood turns brown to begin with and is finally hollowed out. (Agric. Year Book 1900, p. 207).

II. *Trametes pini* causes the heartwood rot (known as "red heart") of pine; the punkiness and perhaps the ring cracks of fir, long leaf, short leaf, and sugar pines; the speckled rot or red heart of Douglas fir; the cork of western hemlock. It is found only in trees over forty years old, usually more in the top of the tree,—but in *Pinus monticola* close to the gound. The wood never rots out entirely and the absence of cavities is characteristic of this fungus. It enters through branch stubs containing heartwood. Reference Bull. For. 33, p. 15, F. & I. 1902, p. 62; Agric Year Book 1900, plate XXII. and XXIV. and page 206.

III. *Polyporus juniperinus* creates long holes coated white in the heartwood of red cedar. (For. Bull. 31, p. 25; Agric. Year Book 1900, p 208; Bull 21 of Div. of Vegetable Pathology).

IV. *Polyporus carneus* causes the red rot of red cedar and of arbor vitæ. The wood splits into small cubes, charcoal like. (Bull. 21 of Div. of Vegetable Physiology and Pathology; For. Bull. 21, p. 26).

V. *Polyporus versicolor* causes the soft rot of live catalpa, *Polyporus catalpæ* the brown rot of the species; Bull. Bureau Plant Industry, No 149, page 47 and pp. 53 to 56; Bull. 37 of Bureau of Forestry, pp 51-58; also in oak and hemlock and beech (For. Bull. 51, p. 31) as a saprophyte on ties.

VI. *Polyporus rimosus* causes the yellow rot of black locust, in its heartwood. Holes made by locust borers (*Cyllene robiniæ*) serve as entrances. (Agric. Year Book 1900, p. 207); Contr. Shaw School of Botany, No. 17; Bureau Plant Industry Bull. No. 149, p 45.

VII. *Polyporus schweinitzii* causes the "butt rot," "ground rot" or "root rot" of all conifers, notably of Douglas fir and hemlock. Fungus enters at the base of the tree through insect mines. Trees die in patches; sporophores are short-lived. (Bull. For. 33, p. 15; F. & I. 1902, p. 61; Agric. Year Book 1900, p.p 203 and 206, and plate XXIV).

VIII. *Polyporus fraxinophilus* occurs in white ash having over seven inches d.b.h. The hyphæ seem to enter by the water niches left by broken branches. Wood becomes straw colored. Very frequent. Reference Bull. 32 and Bull. 149, page 46, of Bureau of Plant Industry.

IX. *Polyporus nigricans* attacks beech, birch and poplar in the New England States causing standing timber to rot. (Agric. Year Book 1900, p. 207; Bulletin Bureau Plant Industry No. 149, p. 42).

X. *Polyporus sulfureus* causes the brown rot of many conifers, also of oak, walnut and cherry. (Bull. Bureau Plant Industry No. 149, page 37; Agric. Year Book 1900, p. 207).

XI. *Polyporus igniarius* occurs everywhere on beech and oak (Agric. Year Book 1900, p 207, Bulletin Bureau Plant Industry, No. 149, pp. 25 to 37).

XII. *Polyporus libocedris* causes the peckiness of bald cypress and the pin rot of incense cedar. The pecks consist of disconnected holes (or pockets) about 4″ long ending abruptly and partially filled with brown powder. Found in trees over 100 years old. Reference. Contr. Shaw School of Botany, No. 14.

XIII. *Polyporus pinicola.* Western conifers, four years after death, are found entirely destroyed by *Polyporus pinicola.* Reference: F. & I., 1902, p. 60; Agric. Year Book 1900, pp. 202 and 209 and plate XXV.

XIV. *Polyporus obtusus* is a common cause of the sap rot in dead oak trees (Bull. Bureau of Plant Industry, p. 41).

XV. *Polyporus fulvus* causes the so-called "red heart" of the birch (Bull. Bureau of Plant Industry, p. 47).

XVI. *Polyporus squamosus* causes "white rot" in various hardwood trees, e. g. maple, oak, beech, birch and ash. (Bull. Bureau of Plant Industry, p. 48).

XVII. *Polyporus pergamenus* causes the "sap rot" of trees and logs—often after fires—in many hardwoods (notably oak); its work is particularly quick, and so is the rapidity of its fruiting (Bull. Bureau of Plant Industry, No 149, p. 56).

XVIII. *Polyporus betulinus* and *fomentarius* may parasitically weaken living birches and beeches (Mayr), or may be satisfied to cause the decomposition of weakened and of dead wood (Von Schrenk). (Bull Bureau of Plant Industry, No. 149, p. 49).

XIX. *Polyporus applanatus* is reported as the killer (?) of cottonwoods (Bull. Bureau of Plant Industry, No. 149, p 58).

XX. *Polyporus ponderosus* n. sp., described in detail by H. von Schrenk in Bull. 36 of Bureau of Plant Industry, p. 37 f.f.g., causes the red rot of *Pinus ponderosa* killed by insect pests at the lapse of two years. The fungus is a saprophyte closely resembling *Polyporus pinicola.*

I. Aside of the *Polypori*, the following technically obnoxious fungi deserve attention.

I. *Lenzites sepiaria* is a saprophyt preying on hemlock, long leaf and short leaf pine—notably on railroad ties. (Reference For. Bull. 51).

II. *Schizophyllum commune* attacks railroad ties of short leaf pine, hemlock, etc. saprophytically. (Ref. For. Bull. 51).

III. Unnamed fungus, the sporophores of which are unknown, attacks *Sequoia sempervirens* and causes "brown rot" (or "butt rot" or "pin rot"), the decay beginning in the inner rings of heartwood near the ground. The fibre is converted into pockets, usually twice as broad as long, filled with dark brown matter. (Reference: For. Bull. 38, pp. 29-31, and plates X. and XI).

IV. *Ceratostomella (Sphæria) pilifera*, a saprophyt of the family *Discomycetes*, causes the bluing of sapwood in the lumber and in the dead boles (killed by *Dendroctonus*) of *Pinus ponderosa.* This fungus does not interfere with the strength of the timber; it decreases its fissibility—a disadvantage in cutting of railroad ties. The spores seem to enter through the ladder mines made by the Ambrosia beetles—but do not seem to develop into Ambrosia. Reference: Bull. 36, Bureau of Plant Industry entire.

"The bluing" of the sapwood in logs and lumber is disastrous notably to the value of poplar logs driven or rafted to destination during spring and summer, of poplar sap lumber, pine saps, sap gum and the like, sawed and slowly air dried during spring and summer. These injuries are due to undescribed fungi.

V. *Echinodontium tinctorium* attacks western hemlock causing "cork,"—like *Trametes pini;* also in spruce and red fir. (Reference. For. Bull. 33, p. 15).

J. General remedies against fungi on live trees.

I. Extermination or removal of the fungus itself;

(1) in case of seeds, by sterilization with hot water, or copper "steep-mixtures."

(2) in case of leaf-fungi, by dusting or spraying with mixtures containing copper or sulphur.

(3) in case of *Agaricaceæ* and *Polyporaceæ*, by removal of sporophores, by excision;

(4) in case of dead parts of plants carrying sporocarps, or other reproductive stages of fungi, by dead-pruning, or removal of dead litter on ground.

II. Extermination of living host or of affected parts of same.

(1) Removal of living host.

(2) Removal of complimentary (heterœcious) host.

III. Avoidance of conditions favoring infection.

(1) no wounds, or antiseptic treatment of same;

(2) avoidance of localities favorable to disease;

(3) no large, even aged, pure forests;

(4) no selection systems, no summer cutting;

(5) rotation of crops;

(6) no planting of heterœcious hosts together;

(7) mixed forests; short rotation; suppression of boring insects; no artificial pruning of living branches;

(8) raising strong trees of individual power of resistence and independent for help from neighbors;

(9) improvement cuttings and thinnings.

K. General remedies against fungi in nurseries.

(1) Change of species, notably in nursery beds.

(2) Sterilized soil in nursery beds.

(3) Deep trenches between nursery beds.

(4) Drenching the beds with a weak solution of sulphuric acid (one ounce of acid to one gallon of water) prior to seed planting and after the sprouting of the seedlings. Compare Circular No. 4, Bureau of Plant Industry.

(5) Production of fungus proof varieties.

(6) Spraying of affected leaves or shoots, or beds with Bordeaux mixture, consisting of a 3% solution of copper sulphate and lime (Recipe, Tubeuf & Smith, page 69).

L. General remedies against fungi in young regenerations.

(1) Use very strong plants.

(2) Do not buy plants from nurseries known to be infested.

(3) Toungya.

(4) Avoid foreigners.

(5) Plant only kinds known to suit the locality.

(6) No regeneration from mother trees in pine (*Hysterium!*) in beech (*Phytophtora!*) etc.

(7) No seedlings of conifers near stumps of hardwoods.

M. General remedies against fungi in lumber, ties and poles.

(1) Wet storage; preservation in ponds (mill), saltwater (tamarack), running water (Cæsar's Rhine bridge), swamps (Ky. walnut).

(2) Dry storage (like furniture) under shelter; dry kiln!!

(3) "Antistain," or "painting," or exposure to sun and wind; or else interruption of logging and milling from April to September.

(4) Impregnation either of the wood, or of the medium in which the wood is kept. (Compare H. von Schrenk, in Bull. 14, Bureau of Plant Industry; further Lectures on "Utilization" by C. A. Schenck, paragraph XLIV).

Par. 8. Protection Against Parasites Other Than Fungi.

A. A number of phanerogams live parasitically upon various trees, notably in the tropics.

In the United States, the common mistletoe (*Phoradendron flavescens*) and the dwarf mistletoe (*Arceuthobium cryptopoda* and *pusillum*) are worthy of note. (Bull. Bureau of Plant Industry No. 149, pp 14 to 17). *Arceuthobium occidentale* deforms the bole and the branches of western hemlock, causing cancerous tumors (Plate VI, Forestry Bulletin No. 33, p. 16).

The damage done by these parasites is so insignificant that remedies are nowhere indicated.

B. Tree mosses, tree algæ and tree lichens are variously reported as malefactors when occurring in such quantities that young leaves and fresh shoots are smothered by them. It is possible also that they interfere with the function of the "lenticels." *Tillandsia usneoides* and *Usnea barbata* may be mentioned as representatives of this group. The former called "Spanish moss" is a flowering plant, common on trees in the Southern States, the latter, a lichen, is abundant in northern swamps and woods Compare Bulletin No. 149, Bureau of Plant Industry, page 17.

Part B: Protection Against Inorganic Nature.

CHAPTER I: PROTECTION AGAINST ADVERSE CLIMATIC INFLUENCES.

Par. 9. Protection Against Frost.

FROST MAY BE BENEFICIAL

By checking insect plagues (late frost), also mice and other rodents, decimating them in cold and protracted winters;

By clipping back inferior species competing with aristocrats (beech vs oak at Viernheim); undesirable coppice sprouts, cut in August, are apt to die;

By furnishing ice on lakes and on iced roads, creating conditions favorable to transportation by sleds, and steady weather for logging, skidding, etc.,

By increasing the value of firewood, and oftentimes by forcing men to take employment in the woods when other occupations are barred by frost.

A. FROST IS INJURIOUS TO UTILIZATION

BY INTERFERING

1. in the south with the logging operations,—owing to the unreliability of the occurrence of frost, the necessity of shoeing cattle, the formation of jams in flumes; the interference by late frost with tan bark peeling, etc.; also by bursting trees, when felled in frozen condition; by toughness of fibre so as to retard the feed of the saw-carriage; by danger to water pipes, connected with engines, boilers, locomotives, donkey engines, etc.; by necessity of changing the setting of the teeth, and the temper and the speed of the saw.
2. in the north with water transportation on the lakes (notably Great Lakes) and rivers (notably St. Lawrence).

B. FROST IS INJURIOUS PHYSIOLOGICALLY (SYLVICULTURALLY)

BY KILLING LEAVES, BUDS, SHOOTS, BRANCHES (notably sappy shoots), flowers and fruits, seedlings and (rarely) saplings.

There is no proof at hand of poles or trees of native species being killed by frost.

Foreigners (e. g., palms, eucalypts and many species tried in northern prairies) are subject to frost.

Absolute cold is not injurious, *eo ipso*, to native species, which know how to protect themselves
by leaves dropped
by non-freezing cell contents
by lignification
by cork layers, bud scales, hairs
by color
by position (rolled up rhododendron leaves)
by beginning growth late and by finishing it early.

The death of a specimen, or of parts of it, is brought about, in all probability, by a rapid transition from cold to warm (cite various theories, and experiments made to support them). Hence it is that the severe frost of winter, or frost occurring at a time at which plants are protected, is less injurious than a light early frost in fall or a light late frost in spring.

Frost occurring unexpectedly is most injurious,—and particularly so to the young parts of an old plant or to a plant, all parts of which are young and tender (e. g., germinating seedlings).

(a) INFLUENCING FACTORS ARE:
Locality (frost holes), latitude, altitude, exposures (eastern),
Atmospheric conditions preceding and following a cold spell,
Snow cover;
Condition of plant (germs sprouting; buds opening; shoots lengthening; lignification unfinished);
Size (age) of plants;
Presence or absence of wind.

(b) CONSEQUENCES OF FROST ARE:
Failures of nursery beds;
Failure of natural seed regenerations,
Failure of seed years;
Failure of seedlings to compete with weeds (e. g., sedgegrass and walnut at Biltmore), and with rabbits (e. g., maple and chestnutoak at Biltmore);
Saplings and seedlings growing bushy or forking (cherry, loosing tips of shoots incessantly; larch, at Biltmore, on Bradley Plantation, due to September frost, 1906; echinata at Biltmore, everywhere, due to September frost, 1906);
Aristocrats smothered by mob (walnut at Biltmore overtopped by hard maple, owing to frost);

Shortened growing season;

Restricted number of species locally producible;

Double rings of wood, and possibly windshakes in wood;

Weakened condition of a tree, subjecting it to insects and fungi, and also to breakage by storm, snow and sleet, owing to the reduced elasticity of the fibre

(c) SPECIES AFFLICTED:

The species known to suffer, in one way or another, from frost are called "sensitive;" the others are known as "hardy" species.

AT BILTMORE

HARDY	SENSITIVE
Chestnut	Beech
Maples	Oaks
Black Gum	Catalpa
Scotch Pine	Oregon Ash
White Pine	Oregon Maple
Rigid Pine	Box Elder
Halesia	Pinus ponderosa
Cottonwood	Pinus lambertiana
Hickories	Pinus echinata
Spruces	Edgeworthia
Douglasia	Walnut
Yellow Poplar	Buckeye

(d) THE REMEDIES AGAINST FROST ARE ALMOST ENTIRELY PREVENTIVE:

(Restrictive measures are possible only in nurseries, and consist in watering the beds after very cold nights).

1. IN NURSERIES:

Late planting of seeds in spring, where late frost is dreaded; or else early planting where early frost is feared in fall;

Lath screens, or nursery under cover (unless lignification is handicapped);

Clouds of smoke on frosty mornings;

Avoidance of east aspects;

Heeling-out transplants, so as to retard sprouting in spring;

Avoidance of dense stands in seed beds (ash seedlings at Biltmore failed to lignify in 1905, excepting those at outer edge).

2. IN PLANTATIONS:

REMARK: A seedling once crippled by frost is apt to be crippled again, and again, and again, owing to the fact, that the replacement of organs once lost takes time; so that the growing season is shortened. The walnuts and buckeyes at Biltmore, once clipped back by frost have been clipped back annually.

Early planting in spring to avoid early frost;

Late planting in spring to avoid late frost;

No experimenting with the introduction of new species;

Natural regeneration of Pinus echinata (also White Pine in Adirondacks) to avoid formation of double whirls;

Planting sensitive species beneath a light cover overhead, so as to prevent excessive height growth, or premature formation of spring shoots.

Use of strong stocky seedlings, since minute plants are prevented from lignification by shading weeds.

Selecting species suiting the soil (walnut on best soil, where it will lignify; echinata on poor soil, where it will form one shoot only), the exposure, and the climate (prairie planting);

Cultivation, so as to stimulate insolation and lignification; possibly pruning to same end; or else to give the lead to one side shoot amongst several when the leader is frost-killed.

3 IN NATURAL SEED REGENERATION:

Progress of the axe in shelterwood-types according to the requirements of the seedlings, viz., slow, where late frost is feared, so as to retard the act of sprouting in spring; or else rapid, where early frost is feared, so as to allow of lignification;

Untimely and sudden removal of mother trees may shock tender plants (even spruce 5′ high), on the other hand.

Frost may be invited on purpose to check a less desirable species in mixture with a hardier and more desirable species.

C. Frost is Injurious

by lifting (uprooting) seedlings in nurseries and plantations.

Subject to damage are:

Flat rooted species growing slowly in early youth, notably conifers (yellow pine yearlings, white pine yearlings, spruce, hemlock);

Moist localities and loose soil;

East exposures, and notably steep east aspects.

(a) Remedial measures are:

Pressing seedlings back, soon after accident.

(b) Restrictive measures are:

1. In nurseries:

Drainage by deep paths (middlings) between the beds;

Proper æration of soil;

Seedbeds planted broadcast;

Strong seedlings, and long roots;

Shading beds, and covering space between the rows of plants;

No weeding in early fall.

2. In plantations

Planting on reversed sods;

Mound planting,

Planting three year-olds (two year old transplants in case of yellow pine);

Planting ball plants;

Planting under shelter overhead.

D. Frost is Injurious

by causing frost cracks

in hardwoods only, notably in case of injured trees and of species having strong medullary rays.

Insect disease and fungus disease follow in the cracks.

Remedy: Timely thinning or improvement cutting.

Cracks occur, notably,

along lower part of bole;

on standards over coppice;

on south side of trees;

on medium sized trees (1½′-3′).

in moist localities

Par. 10. Protection Against Heat.

A. Heat Causes Harm Only:

When it invites forest fires;

When it fails to be balanced by the moisture in the air or soil (wood lots in the prairies; old park trees);

When it occurs suddenly, striking the trees in a state of non-protection (e. g., new plantations and trees isolated of a sudden).

B. The Plants Protect Themselves Ordinarily Against Heat:

By dropping leaves;

By resinous cell contents;

By closed stomata;

By color and position of leaves;

By coverings of cork, hair and that like.

C. Remedies:

1. In infant forests.

(a) in nurseries.

Secure irrigation;

Provide lath screens or cloth screens;

Maintain a cover of mould on the soil;

Cultivate so as to increase the porosity of soil;

Plant the seeds early in spring before the winter moisture has vanished;

Transplant early and transplant deeply.

(b) in plantations:

Use strong transplants;

Adopt mound planting;

Plant under cover;

Adopt ball planting;

Avoid loss of root fibres during act of out-planting;

Cultivate.

(c) in natural seed regenerations:

Remove mother trees slowly;

Remove trees reflecting heat unto young growth.

(d) Generally.

Maintain a dense cover overhead, and a good layer of humus underneath.

2. In pole forests and tree forests:

Characteristic for damage (so-called sunscald) is:

Bark scaling off;

Sap wood turning brown;

Discoloration and decay within a distinct sector of bole.

(a) Prevent sunscald by avoiding sudden changes of the influx of light;

Notably so in the case of dense stands of beech, spruce, white pine, ash;

Notably on the West-South-West edge of a wood lot.

At Biltmore, Oak saplings along the macadamized roads; chestnuts on the arboretum road; and hickories of small diameter have been visited by the disease.

(b) Do not remove the trees affected by sunscald; their removal will merely expose the trees in the rear, and the damage will continue.

(c) Do not remove, from endangered trees, by pruning, any living branches.

(d) Time the progress of the axe properly in thinnings, preparatory cuttings, seed cuttings and removal cuttings.

Par. 11. Protection Against Snow and Sleet.

SNOW IS BENEFICIAL:

By preventing fires;
By storing water and by preserving soil moisture;
By facilitating the logging operations;
By covering sensitive plants;
By removing dead side branches;
By preventing frost from entering deeply into soil;
By reducing the felling damages.

A. SNOW IS TECHNICALLY OBNOXIOUS:

By preventing the use of wagons or railroads;
By endangering skidding on steep slopes;
By increasing sledding expenses (when snow is too deep);
By causing extra outlay in cutting stumps low to the ground;
By reducing the accessibility of the woods.
Remark. Winters of excessive snow are known as winters of restricted output of lumber.

B. SNOW IS PHYSIOLOGICALLY OBNOXIOUS:

By bending down saplings and poles with or without their roots;
By breaking off branches and crowns or by breaking down poles and trees with the roots;
By causing rodents and game to attack trees and saplings for food;
By exposing trees after breakage to the attacks of insects and fungi;
By increasing storm damage at a time when the trees are loaded with snow or sleet.

C. FACTORS OF DAMAGE.

Species and mixture of species;
Age and size of trees;
Method of regeneration and notably the density thereof;
Climatic constellations (e. g., coincidence of storm, succession of thaws and snows; occurrences of snow in Octover, before the fall of the leaves);
Preceding treatment by thinning; by removal cuttings; by leaving standards after coppiceing; by road making.
Locality, elevation and aspect.
Steepness of slope;
Depth of soil (Coxehill);
Rate of growth (fast grown yellow pine and top whirls of fast grown white pine at Biltmore;)
Prior injuries by fire, by boxing, by insects and fungi (black locusts).

Remark. Remember the following illustrations.
White cedar in swamps of South Carolina;
Cuban pine in Alabama;

Poplar tops in Pisgah Forest;
Topped white pines in the Pink Beds;
Black locusts and hickory on mountain tops;
Plantations of rigid pine in Black Forest;
Spruce saplings in the Balsams, in the early spring of 1908.

D. REMEDIES:

Selecting the proper species for planting or for natural seed regenerations, in keeping with the requirements of the locality and of the climate;
Group system of natural seed regeneration;
Planting in rows instead of planting in triangles (Hess);
Thinnings properly made beginning early in very dense regenerations;
Pollarding;
Readiness of permanent means of transportation so as to make possible the salvage of broken timber.

CHAPTER II: PROTECTION AGAINST STORM, EROSION, SANDDRIFTS, NOXIOUS GASES.

Part 12. Protection Against Wind Storms.

WIND IS BENEFICIAL:

By restoring the chemical balance of the atmosphere;
By distributing pollen and seeds;
By preventing excessive formation of side branches;
By bringing rain.

A. DAMAGE IS CAUSED BY WIND STORM (aside of forest fires spread or fanned):

(a) IN PLANTATIONS:

By loosening the anchorage of tall seedlings and saplings, (notably, after planting in furrows, in the prairies, on sand dunes);
By drying out roots and shoots and leaves and soil (notably in the early spring);
By removing the protecting cover of snow;
By allowing the "mob" to whip the top shoots of "aristocrats."

(b) IN EXPOSED LOCALITIES:

By one-sided (seashore or Pisgah ridge) or stunted growth.

(c) IN TREE FORESTS AND IN LARGE POLE WOODS:

By breakage of crowns or branches, thus allowing access to fungi and to insects;
By breakage of stems at their point of least resistence;
By uprooting trees singly, in avenues, or in large blocks;
By endangering the logging operations.

B. FACTORS OF DAMAGE ARE:

(a) SPECIES:

Flat-rooted conifers are most endangered; a mixture of species in advisable.

(b) SIZE CLASS:

Poles and trees over 8″ in diameter are most subject to damage.

(c) LOCALITY:

Leeward sides of lakes;
Mountain slopes and mountain tops on leeward side;
Moist spots;
Shallow soil.

(d) Prior Treatment:

Partial logging, leaving a freshly bared front exposed to the prevailing storm;
Standards over coppice;
Single seedtrees over regeneration;
Borggreve thinnings;
Turpentining by the box system;
Interference with anchorage of roots by making ditches or roads.

(e) Shape of trees:

Cylindrical trees are more top heavy than conical trees.

(f) Accompanying circumstances:

Heavy rains soaking the soil;
Heavy seed years when the tops of the trees are loaded with cones;
Sleet;
Snow.

C. Preventive measures:

(a) Sylviculturally:

Ball planting, deep planting, sod covering on shifting sand.
Fostering hardwoods or mixture therewith;
Early and moderate and regular thinnings;
Pruning or lopping to reduce top-heaviness;
No standards,
No single tree method of natural seed regeneration;
Proper preparation in due time of trees intended for an isolated position;
Short rotations.

(b) Technically:

Avoidance of logging methods leaving points favorable to the attack of storms;
Progress of the axe against the direction of the barometric minima;
Herty method of terpentining;
Proper "cutting series;"
Timely "severance cuttings."

D. Restrictive Measures:

Readiness of means of transportation (railroads and roads) after wind falls;
Removing the bark from wind falls;
Throwing wind falls in water.

Par. 13. Protection Against Erosion.

The adult forest does not require any protection from erosion—usually so.

It must be remembered, on the other hand, that "civilization" (by ditching the slopes on the hills, by cutting roads and railroads into the soil; by draining the bottom-lands for farming purposes) increases the rapidity of the subterranean and of the superficial drainage, that it results in a partial destruction of the soil on the hill sides.

Erosion, in the present geological aera, is not so active, nevertheless, as it was in prior periods.

A forest plantation on the hill side suffers during its early stages from erosion where the soil consists of clay, and where the plough has preceded the establishment of the embryo-forest.

Some seedlings are washed out of the soil whilst others are covered by detritus.

At Biltmore, erosion has harmed particularly the so-called "old school house" plantation, in its earliest stage of development.

As soon as the forest covers the ground fully, viz.: when the branches of neighboring specimens interlace, all erosion is usually stopped and stopped for good.

Oftentimes deep gullies are cut into the side slopes during and after agricultural occupancy of the soil; in such cases, the stopping of the gullies by wicker works or hurdles can be recommended.

These wicker works should not protrude more than one-half foot above the surface of the soil.

They should be made, particularly, at the upper end of the gully. It is useless to make them at the lower end alone.

These wicker works will hinder erosion to a certain extent; will quiet the soil within the gully; and will allow the grasses and the weeds to occupy the sides of the gully

The most interesting case of erosion met in Eastern America is, possibly, the erosion exhibited in the immediate proximity of the smelter works at Ducktown, Tenn.

Here, the hillsides were laid bare entirely at a time at which the smelters used the timber for charcoal

Following this deforestation, the bared areas were used for roasting (by the open heap method) of the copper-bearing ores. As a consequence, every vestige of vegetation has been annihilated on the hillsides and erosion has had a chance to work in an amazing degree of intensity.

Erosion may be checked by horizontal ditches—or ditches running at a very light grade; by the planting of grasses or weeds between horizontal ditches; and finally, by afforestation.

There is no means better than successful afforestation by which the soil can be fastened or anchored to the underlying rock.

Afforestation as a topic of lectures belongs into "Sylviculture" and into "Forest Policy."

Par. 14. Protection Against Shifting Sands.

Instances are rare in which the forest requires any protection against shifting sands.

On the other hand, the forest frequently tends to protect from damage the farms, the railroads and other human interests.

In other words: The forest requires, rarely, protection against shifting sands; and it acts frequently as a protector against shifting sands.

Famous instances of the role which the forest plays in this connection are those of Cape Cod, Mass.; of Hatteras Island, N. C. (Compare Collier Cobb's article in the National Geographic Magazine entitled "Where the wind does the work"); in Central Hungary; in the Landes of Gascogny, France; in the Rhine Valley near Darmstadt, Germany; along the Columbia River in Oregon and Washington; and so on).

A. Shifting sand along the seashore is found notably in the form of sand dunes moving landward, fed and driven by ocean winds.

It would be unwise to attempt any afforestation of the dunes nearest the ocean. Afforestation may set in at some distance from the ocean in protected depressions found between parallel dunes.

The dunes are fixed, to begin with, by rough palings forming the heart of the dunes and causing a constant growth of the height of the dunes. The sides of the dunes are fortified by sandgrasses and sandweeds.

The species used for afforestation belong to particularly modest genera: Cottonwoods, willows and pines are recommended.

Obviously, the forester restocking shifting sands is interested in the fixation of the sands more than in a direct revenue derivable from plantations made at a very high expense on very sterile soil.

B. The case lies somewhat different on sand areas found inland. Here, afforestation is frequently indicated as a means toward a revenue obtainable from soil lying otherwise unproductive and threatening, at the margins of the sand fields, destruction to adjoining farmland.

The usual method of proceeding is the following:

Sods of grasses or else sods of heather are laid on the soil, checker-board fashion. Within the sods are planted longrooted yellow pines, preference being given to transplants two years old or else to ball plants one year old. There is no harm in "deep planting."

Afforestation should begin on the windward side of the sand area, in protected spots

The most famous attempt made in America toward the afforestation of inland sands is that of the Forest Service trying to establish, on the "Bad Lands" of Nebraska, a planted forest on a large scale.

It is obvious that small plants are pulled out of a loose soil readily by the wind—notably so in the case of evergreens; and that large transplants suffer badly from the shock of outplanting and from the inadequacy of the water supply available on sterile sand.

Wheresoever the soil is apt to become shifting, the law should prohibit the removal of the trees by their owners.

The influence in that direction exercised by a commonwealth is dealt with in the lectures on "Forest Policy."

Par. 15. Protection Against Noxious Gases (Sulphurfumes).

By the term "sulphurfumes" are understood certain gases formed by the oxidation of sulphur. Huge amounts of these gases are produced wherever sulphur-bearing minerals are treated in the presence of atmospheric air.

Contamination of the atmosphere is one of the evils adherent to civilization, or, which is the same, adherent to an increase of population at certain centers. The breath of any man or any animal and, more than that, the smoke rising from any building (dwellings as well as factories) contaminate the air.

After Angus Smith, the atmosphere at Manchester, England, contains a little less than the one-millionth part of SO_2 on the average of the year.

The rain water investigations made by the same English author show the rapid increase of sulphuric acid in rain water near industrial centers.

The sulphur contained in common coal averages 1.7%, of which 1.2% develop into noxious sulphurfumes. In other words, 85 tons of coal will develop on the average 2 tons of noxious SO_2.

Since the consumption of bituminous coal in the United States is in excess of 200,000,000 tons per annum, it appears that we send into the atmosphere (pre-eminently in the northeast) annually about 4,700,000 tons of sulphurous acid.

A. Nature of Damage to Leaves.

There is not at hand, at the present time, any scientific explanation of the strange physiological effect which sulphur fumes exercise upon vegetation.

After Prof. Naegeli, SO_2 checks the normal movement of the live plasma in the leaves.

Von Schroeder finds that the transpiration from the leaves is that function which is most vitally reduced by inhalation of SO_2.

During night, transpiration from the leaves is naturally reduced to a minimum, and it is interesting to note that there is little difference in the evaporative function of leaves during night, whether they be exposed to SO_2 or whether they be left in an atmosphere free from SO_2.

When the sun shines, the difference between the evaporation in leaves exposed to SO_2 and in leaves exposed to a pure atmosphere is very striking.

Reduced transpiration appears to be noticeable before discoloration of leaves occurs in a sulphurous atmosphere.

After von Schroeder, very small quantities of SO_2 continuously acting produce the same final result (always in the glass case) which large quantities will produce acting for short periods only. This observation does not tally with the results of Freytag's experiments made in the open air.

Darkness reduces the damage by SO_2 more than dryness. In the presence of light, heat and humidity, the discoloring and deadening action of SO_2 is most intense; which is to say: It is strongest when the vital functions of the leaves are most active.

Parallel experiments show no discoloration as a consequence of the absorption of SO_2 in the dark room (at night), although such absorption takes place actually.

Wet leaves show much more discoloration than dry leaves in the same sulphurous atmosphere.

The main difficulty met in ascertaining the dilution at which SO_2 becomes innocuous lies in the disturbing influence of light and moisture.

After Freytag (experiments in the open air) damage is possible only in humid air, or when the leaves are slightly wet from drizzling rain and from dew.

Again, after Freytag, air containing less than 0.003% (of weight) of SO_2 is innocuous, even under adverse hydrographic conditions and in spite of continuous fumigation, applied during a number of weeks.

Freytag's experiments are the only open-air experiments which have been conducted with scientific correctness.

SO_2 and SO_3 are absorbed in the same absolute quantities by the leaves when present in the air in equal proportions. Discoloration of leaves, however, and decrease in transpiration from leaves are, simultaneously, much smaller in an atmosphere of SO_3 than in an atmosphere of SO_2. Consequently, all conditions which favor the formation of SO_3 in the air before the air touches the leaves must decrease the damage—especially so in the case of chronic affections.

The assumption that clouds of smoke interfere with the admission of light and hence with the assimilation of the leaves is erroneous.

There is no such thing as the "stuffing up" of the so-called stomata found on the leaves (through which inhalation and transpiration takes place) caused by soot or solid particles contained in the fumes.

Experiments made by Stoeckhardt prove this thesis beyond a doubt.

B. Chemical Remarks.

Sulphurous acid (H_2SO_3) is unknown in the free state; it is likely to be contained in the solution of gaseous SO_2 in the water.

Sulphurous acid forms primary and secondary sulphites; its salts are obtained by saturating a base with a watery solution of SO_2.

If sulphurous acid is eliminated from its salts by the action of stronger acids, then it forms its anhydrid and water.

Since a large number of calories of heat are set free by the union of S and O, in forming the SO_2, the anhydrid is a constant combination.

SO_2 is readily reduced, by H_2S, into water and sulphur.

In watery solutions as well as in gaseous form SO_2 readily oxidises into SO_3, when exposed to the influence of the atmosphere, 32 calories of heat being liberated by such oxidation.

On the other hand, SO_3 at red heat dissolves into oxygen and SO_2. It stands to reason that with increasing distance from the smoke-stack the contents of the smoke are more SO_3 than SO_2.

After von Schroeder, the gases of SO_3 are, without a doubt, less damaging to vegetation inhaling them than the gases of SO_2.

Within the leaves SO_2 is very quickly converted, by oxidation, into SO_3.

A few hours after gas-poisoning, only SO_3 (not SO_2) can be proven to be present within the leaves.

Chemical analysis of leaves can only fix the territory infested in a random way. It can never be used as a measure of damage locally found. The damage can be assessed only according to the effects discernible with the naked eye. So-called "invisible damages" have never been allowed by the Courts.

The chemical analysis of leaves suspected to be poisoned deals only with an abnormal (unnatural) surplus of SO_3.

All leaves contain, in nature, certain amounts of SO_3, the amounts depending on the composition of the soil and on the species.

Hence a comparative analysis of the leaves is absolutely necessary where it is intended to establish the influence of sulphurfumes on vegetation. This analysis must allow for the difference in the soil and the difference in the distance from the smelters. At the same time, the leaves examined must be taken from the same part of the tree and from the same side of the tree; further, the leaves must be in the same stage of development.

After recent experiments the sulphuric contents in the leaves within the lower part of the crown are much higher than the sulphuric contents in the upper part of the crown.

The ashes obtained from trees growing in low lands are relatively poorer in SO_3 than the ashes from trees growing on mountains. Weak limbs show more SO_3 than strong limbs.

C THE MERITS OF THE CHEMICAL ANALYSIS.

Science has not established any *absolutely* reliable means to connect death or injury of trees with a poisoning effect of SO_2 or SO_3 suspended in the air surrounding such trees.

An anatomic—microscopic proof of injury due to SO_2 or SO_3 cannot be given (Haselhoff and Lindau, p 93 and p. 37).

A number of injurious influences (frost, heat, desiccation of soil, insects, fungi (Schroeder and Reuss, p. 110) fire, etc.) bring about, within the leaves and needles, identical or similar alterations of the cell-structure (Haselhoff and Lindau, p. 12 ff).

The consensus of opinion, amongst scientific specialists (R. Hartig, p 6; Winkler, p. 379; Schroeder and Reuss, p 126) is to the effect that excessive contents of SO_3 within the leaves are not necessarily injurious.

Injury due to sulphurfumes can be assumed *only* when there are at hand

A. death visible to the naked eye;

B. no other plausible cause of such death;

C. contents of SO_3 in the leaves which are *unmistakably increased* by the reaction of the leaves and needles on sulphur fumes.

UNMISTAKABLY INCREASED contents of SO_3 proven chemically within the leaves are

a. *not* identical with *abnormal* contents;

b. *not* such contents as exceed the average contents of leaves within territories acknowledged to be beyond the reach of sulphur fumes; in other words,

c. *not* particularly high percentages of SO_3 found within the leaves. General averages holding good for the contents of SO_3 within the leaves of healthy trees do not exist (Haselhoff and L ndau, p. 67).

If the contents of SO_3 found within the injured or uninjured leaves and needles of a given tree exceed those obtained by averaging a large number of analytic results obtained from the tests of healthy leaves and needles, then and in such case the *excess* is frequently due to any one, or to a combination of the following causes:

(a) SOIL: A *soil* naturally rich in SO_3 or irrigated with water containing SO_3, produces leaves and needles *surcharged* with SO_3. Such surcharge has *no* detrimental influence on the state of health of the trees (Haselhoff and Lindau, p. 46, p. 51, p. 55, p. 56).

(b) AGE. Old needles contain more SO_3 than young needles. (Haselhoff and Lindau, p. 67; Schroeder and Reuss, p. 128).

(c) SEASON. Young leaves contain more SO_3 than old leaves.

(d) POSITION: On the same healthy tree, the sulphur contents of the leaves *vary* according to the position of the leaves, which position might be

at the base or at the top of the crown,
on the inside or on the outside of the crown.

(e) ELEVATION: On the slope of a hill, the sulphur contents in the healthy leaves of the same tree-species exhibit variations depending on the elevation above sea-level (Schroeder and Reuss, p. 126).

The sulphur contents of given leaves and needles are "*unmistakably increased*" by the reaction on sulphur fumes in all cases where it can be proven that none of the causes of increase above enumerated has or have brought about such increase. It is advisable, as a consequence,

(1) to back the chemical analysis of the leaves by the chemical analysis of the soil on which such leaves were produced, so as to prove that an in-

crease of leaf-sulphur is not due to an increase of soil-sulphur (Haselhoff and Lindau, p. 378);

(2) to compare the analytic results of such leaves and needles only which were picked

- *equally* old;
- *equally* situated within the crown of the trees;
- *equally* situated with reference to elevation.

All experts agree that short, sudden, strong attacks by sulphur fumes are apt to be deadly; still, such attacks do not cause a VERY MARKED increase of SO_3 in the leaves.

On the other hand, long-continued, but slight attacks by sulphur fumes result in a heavy increase of SO_3 in the leaves; still, such attacks do not cause a *very marked* injury to the trees (Wislicenus, Journal of Applied Chemistry, 1901, p. 28).

It is evident, consequently, that conclusions based on the chemical analysis of leaves and needles are apt to be rash; and that so-called chemical proofs must be viewed with great precaution (Wieler, p. 380).

D. UNRELIABILITY OF GLASS-CASE EXPERIMENTS.

Experiments touching the poisonous effect of fumes made with plants placed in a glass case cannot be so telling as experiments made in the open, because:

a. In the glass case, the gas is admitted from below so as to infest the lower surface of the leaves, which lower surface is known to be more subject to sulphur attacks than the upper surface.

b. Sulphurous anhydrid, in statu nascendi, is increasingly active and pre-eminently corrosive.

c. The discoloration of the leaves in nature differs from the discoloration usually observed in glass case experiments.

d. In nature, SO_3 is largely mixed with SO_2, the former being less active than the latter. In the glass case, usually, only SO_2 is developed.

E. Factors of Damage.

Without a doubt, a slight admixture to the atmosphere of either SO_2 or SO_3 has a certain influence on vegetation; such influence being irregularly proportioned to the amount of the admixture.

After Stoeckhardt, the one-millionth part of the air consisting of SO_3 results, in the course of time, in discoloration (335 fumigations discolor wet leaves in six weeks, dry leaves in eight weeks).

The degree of injury depends on

a. The continuity of the fumigation which is governed by the steadiness of the wind direction and which decreases, step by step, with increasing distance from the smelters.

b. The sensitiveness of the plants which is governed by species, quality of the soil, preceding injury by fire, pasture or general neglect.

c. The number of months per annum during which the leaves show physical activity. In the case of hardwoods, this number is about 3½, extending from May 1 to August 15.

d. Atmospheric conditions which may allow the gases to remain in bulk after emission from the smokestack, thus concentrating the damage on such parts of the country toward which the smoke happens to drift in bulk.

It has been proven by experiments as well as by the experience of all observers in nature, that days of great atmospheric humidity, days on which fog forms and days following nights of heavy dew are particularly prolific in breeding acute discoloration or damage. On the other hand, very bright weather as well as heavy rains seem to minimize the damage by intensive dilution and may prevent damage entirely.

The toxic influence of sulphur gases might be considered either as an acute or as a chronic disease. Acute cases appear only in the near proximity of smelters where clouds of smoke kept in bulk under certain atmospheric constellations actually exercise a corroding influence on the leaves.

On the other hand, where the diluted gases are inhaled by the plants during a long number of days under the influence of a steady wind, there chronic discoloration and chronic disease will enter an appearance.

F. Damage to the Soil.

Conclusive experiments prove that soluble sulphuric salts of copper (like blue vitriol) fail to cause any damage to the plants, whether applied in the form of dust or in the form of watery solution. Very concentrated solutions, however, cause corrosion; also dust falling on leaves wet with dew.

Although the roots of plants are unable to refuse entrance to damaging liquids, it has been found that soluble salts of copper, when entering the soil, form at once an insoluble chemical combination with the bases of the soil. It is possible, however, that poor quartz-sand, in the immediate proximity of the smelters, can be affected by soluble salts of copper.

Insoluble salts of copper are, obviously, harmless in the soil.

Absolute proof for or against soil-poisoning can be obtained only by planting seeds and seedlings into soil supposed to be poisoned, after removal to a point far from the smelters. Planting experiments made by Reuss have failed to prove any posioning of the soil, even under extreme conditions.

The sulphuric acid contained in the soil is by no means proportioned to the damage appearing in the trees. On the other hand, trees stocking on sulphuric soil (e. g. gypsum soil) show invariably a high percentage of sulphuric acid within the leaves. It seems as if sulphuric acid obtained through the roots is innocuous, whilst sulphuric acid inhaled through the leaves is noxious.

If by condensation of the gases at the smelters the atmosphere is purified, the soil in the proximity of the smelters is as ready to produce as ever. In other words, there is no such thing as irreparable damage caused by smelterfumes.

Experiments with plants watered with a solution of SO_2 prove conclusively that no damage results from such watering. On the contrary! After Freytag, plants watered with a solution of SO_2 have shown better yields than those which were not watered with SO_2.

In other words, sulphuric acid has a chance to become a blessing to agriculture, especially where the soil contains insoluble phosphates; and there is, decidedly, no such thing as the "poisoning of the soil" through SO_2 or SO_3, applied in gaseous form or liquid form, as salt or acid.

G. Damage to Farm Crops and Fruit Trees.

Within the vegetation economically used, farm crops suffer less from fumes than trees. In the case of farm crops potatoes seem to be least sensitive, cereals follow next, whilst leguminous plants are more sensitive.

Farming can be carried on remuneratively in closer proximity of the smelters than forestry. Obviously, in the case of annual plants, there is no cumulative influence of SO_2 due to many a year's exposure.

The fact that farm crops are more resistant to smoke than forest crops may be explained ,also, by the higher reproductive power of the former and by the greater height of the latter, the leaves of which are exposed to more concentrated gases of SO_2.

In case of fruit trees, mulberries seem to be least sensitive; then follow apples, pears, peaches, plums, with cherries as the most sensitive fruit trees at the rear end.

Wherever fruit trees are well attended by cultivation and by fertilizing, the damage by sulphur fumes is minimized.

The "floral organs" of the fruit trees seem to be less affected by smoke than the "pulmonary organs," which means to say the fruiting of the trees is not badly interfered with by SO_2 and SO_3.

H. Damage to Forests.

The forest trees, according to species and individuality, exhibit a very varying degree of sensitiveness to the influence of sulphur fumes. The degree of liability to damage is in no way proportioned to the readiness with which the trees inhale sulphuric fumes. For instance, the conifers are more affected by sulphur fumes than are the hardwoods. Still, exposed to the same atmosphere charged with sulphuric fumes, the conifers will inhale smaller quantities of toxic gases than the hardwoods.

The power of resistence which the various species show to the influence of sulphur fumes is, on the other hand, directly proportioned to the power of reproduction (power of recovery) which the various species show. It is obvious that this power of recovery is particularly good in hardwoods, which must recover, every spring, from the natural loss of foliage sustained in the preceding fall.

In the case of broad-leaved species, any loss of vital organs is readily made up, whilst in the case of conifers the reproductive power is comparatively low.

Amongst the conifers, those which retain their needles for a number of years are more apt to suffer from sulphuric fumes than those which retain their needles for one or two years only.

Inasmuch as the resistence which the trees offer to injury by sulphurfumes is proprotioned to their power of reproduction, and inasmuch as this power of reproduction largely depends on the fertility of the soil, it is obvious that all species succumb on impoverished soil more rapidly than on good soil.

This observation is backed by the facts exhibited near Ducktown, Tenn., where the shade trees in the gardens seem to do remarkably well in close proximity to the smelters.

Ceteris paribus, the following schedule has been arranged as the result of investigations for the trees in the Ducktown region having over 7″ diameter, the trees most easily killed by SO_2 being placed at the top of the schedule:

SUSCEPTIBILITY TO ACTUAL INJURY.

White Pine
Hemlock
Scrub Pine
Pitch Pine
Birch
Chestnut
Hickory
Oaks
Yellow Poplar
Maple
Black Gum

This schedule tallies well with the schedule given by European authors for closely related species.

If a similar schedule is formed according to the ease of discoloration, entirely different results are obtained:

SUSCEPTIBILITY TO DISCOLORATION.

VERY EASILY DISCOLORED	MEDIUM DISCOLORED	NOT APT TO BE DISCOLORED
Black Oak	Poplar	Black Gum
Hickory	White Oak	White Pine
Scarlet Oak	Chestnut Oak	Maple
Chestnut	Post Oak	Pitch Pine
Spanish Oak		Hemlock

Noteworthy it is that the power of resistance to fumes is more increased by the power of reproduction than decreased by the sensitiveness of the leaves.

In nature, wherever grave deviations from exact schedules of sensitiveness are found, it stands to reason that other influences, aside from sulphurfumes, are simultaneously responsible for the death or for the discoloration of the trees.

The best time for any observations in the forest is the late summer or early fall (the time between August 15 and October 1).

Sulphurfumes cannot be held responsible for the local death of trees within a "smoke region,"

(1) if species known to be more sensitive are less affected than species known to be more resistent;

(2) if tall specimens are no more affected than short specimens; or if the trees die from below;

(3) if the dying trees are affected with a fungus-disease (e. g. White Pine blight and Chestnut blight) or an insect disease causing the death of the trees outside the smoke region;

(4) if death and discoloration are confined to one species only;

(5) if the owner of the forests, allowing indiscriminate logging, or allowing forest fires to rage, is guilty of contributory negligence;

(6) if discoloration is caused by late frost, or draught, or leaf fungi;

(7) if the death rate within the smoke region is no greater than the death rate without, under otherwise equal conditions (of geology, soil-fertility, aspect, forest fires, desiccation, storms, insects, fungi and prior treatment of forests);

(8) if dying and living trees are normally covered with tree mosses, algæ and lichens;

(9) if the death rate at the windward edge of the forests is not larger than the death rate in the interior;

(10) if the size of the annual rings of accretion is not abnormally small;

(11) if there are at hand, in the affected region, other plausible causes of discoloration and of death.

I. Preventive Measures.

1. In the source of damage:

(a) Dilution of fumes

by emission into the upper atmosphere from mountain tops or from high smoke-stacks;

by accelerated conversion of SO_2 into SO_3;

by artificial draught increasing the rapidity of dilution;

by manufacture of sulphuric acid.

(b) Other means suggested:

by running smelter plants at night (possible in pygmean operations only);

by discontinuing operations in May, June and July (impossible where hundreds of workmen depend on continued employment);

by smelting in the regions where the hardwoods prevail; where the forest has little value; on islands, in deserts or prairies.

2. In woodlands adjoining:
   - (a) Conversion of woodlands into farms or pastures; or of high forest into low forest;
   - (b) Cutting affected and dying trees;
   - (c) Maintaining the fertility and, notably, the water contents of the soil through protection from fire and by keeping a dense undergrowth;
   - (d) Avoidance of partial logging.

I. Index to Malefactors.

II. Index of Species Affected.

Printed in the USA
CPSIA information can be obtained
at www.ICGtesting.com
LVHW050213011224
797933LV00003B/672